Thirty Years With

MASTER NUNO OLIVEIRA:

Correspondence, Photographs and Notes

Chronicled by Michel Henriquet

With a Preface

By Professor Jaime Celestino da Costa

Translated to English

By Hilda Nelson

© Xenophon Press 2011

Xenophon Press Library

A Rider's Survival From Tyranny, Charles de Kunffy 2012
Another Horsemanship, Jean-Claude Racinet, 1994
Art of the Lusitano, Pedro Yglesias de Oliveira 2012
Baucher and His School, General Decarpentry 2011
Dressage in the French Tradition, Dom Diogo de Bragança 2011
Equine Osteopathy: What the Horses have Told me, D. Giniaux, D.V.M. 2014
François Baucher: The Man and His Method, Hilda Nelson 2013
From the Real Picaria of the 18th Century to the Portuguese School of Equestrian Art, Yglesias de Oliveira and da Costa 2012
H. Dv. 12 German Cavalry Manual on Training of Horse and Rider, Reinhold 2014
Healing Hands, Dominique Giniaux, DVM 1998
Horse Training: Outdoors and High School, Étienne Beudant 2014
Methodical Dressage of the Riding Horse, and *Dressage of the Outdoor Horse,* Faverot de Kerbrech 2010
Racinet Explains Baucher, Jean-Claude Racinet 1997
École de Cavalerie Part II (School of Horsemanship), F. R. de la Guérinière 1992
The Écuyères of the Nineteenth Century in the Circus, Hilda Nelson 2001
The Ethics and Passions of Dressage Expanded Edition, Charles de Kunffy 2013
The Gymnasium of the Horse, Gustav Steinbrecht 2011
The Italian Tradition of Equestrian Art, G.B. Tomassini 2014
The Legacy of Master Nuno Oliveira, Stephanie Millham 2013
The Maneige Royal, Antoine de Pluvinel 2010
The Spanish Riding School in Vienna and Piaffe and Passage, General Decarpentry 2013
The Science and Art of Riding in Lightness, Robert Stodulka D.V.M. 2015
The Wisdom of Master Nuno Oliveira, Antoine de Coux 2012
Total Horsemanship, Jean-Claude Racinet 1999
Available at **www.XenophonPress.com**

Title: 30 Years with Master Nuno Oliveira
Copyright © 2011 by Xenophon Press LLC

Translated by Hilda Nelson
Edited by Richard and Frances Williams
All rights reserved. No part of this work may be reproduced or transmitted in any form or by any means, electronic or mechanical, including photocopying, or by any information storage or retrieval system except by a written permission from the publisher.

Published by Xenophon Press LLC, XenophonPress@gmail.com

e-book ISBN   9780933316553

PRINT ISBN   9780933316249

TABLE OF CONTENTS

INTRODUCTION TO THE ENGLISH EDITION iii
TRANSLATOR'S NOTE by Hilda Nelson iv
PREFACE by Jaime Celestino da Costa 1
INTRODUCTION by Michel Henriquet 17
1. Letter: ADDRESSING A FRENCH DISCIPLE 30
2. Letter: PREPARING THE PASSAGE 33
3. Letter: SUPPLING IN THE FORWARD MOVEMENT 35
4. Letter: WORK ON THE LUNGE LINE 37
5. Letter: ELEVATION OF THE NECK 39
6. Note: SOME INTERESTING EXERCISES 41
7. Letter: PREPARATION FOR LEAD CHANGES 42
8. Letter: DEVELOPING THE PASSAGE 43
9. Note: WORK IN HAND 46
10. Letter: TWO TYPES OF RIDERS 47
11. Note: WORKING WITH VARIOUS HORSES 48
12. Letter: THE PASSING OF A BAUCHERIST 50
13. Note: WORKING WITH *VALIOSO* 52
14. Letter: BIOGRAPHY 52
15. Note: A SHOULDER-IN LESSON 54
16. Letter: TWO FRENCH RIDERS 55
17. Note: STUDY OF PASSAGE AND PIAFFE 58
18. Letter: ADVICE ON THE PASSAGE 60
19. Note: REMARKS BY THE MASTER 63
20. Letter: MISUNDERSTANDINGS 64
21. Note: A YOUNG HORSE RUSHING AT THE CANTER 69
22. Letter: CRITICS 70
23. Note: SEEKING THE *RASSEMBLER* 73
24. Letter: PRESENTATIONS IN ENGLAND 75
25. Letter 76
26. Note: ADDRESSING LEANING ON THE SHOULDERS 77
27. Letter: THE RIDER'S SEAT 78
28. Letter: FLYING CHANGES 79
29. Note: PREPARING A FIVE YEAR OLD 81
30. Letter: IMPULSION 83
31. Letter 84
32. Note: ADDRESSING HEAD TOSSING 86
33. Letter 87
34. Note: COPING WITH WEIGHT RESISTANCE IN THE HAND 90
35. Letter: BAUCHER AND THE SCHOOL OF VERSAILLES 91
36. Note: YIELDING OF THE JAW 94

i

37. Letter	96
38. Note: TRAINING FLYING CHANGES	99
39. Letter: LEAD CHANGES FROM RIGHT TO LEFT	100
40. Note: EXERCISE FOR A FOUR-YEAR-OLD HORSE	102
41. Letter: THE IDEAL OF *HAUTE ÉCOLE*	105
42. Note	106
43. Letter: PROGRAM FOR YOUR RIGID THOROUGHBRED	106
44. Note: WORK WITH A FOUR-YEAR-OLD THOROUGHBRED	108
45. Letter: WORDS OF A CRITIC	109
46. Note: REMARKS	112
47. Letter	114
48. Note: WORKING WITH VARIOUS HORSES	115
49. Letter	117
50. Note: WORK IN HAND	118
51. Letter: ACADEMIC EQUITATION OF THE ELDERS	119
52. Letter: BE AN ARTIST, NOT A FIGHTER	121
53. Note: *CURIOSO,* SIX MONTHS OF SCHOOLING	123
54. Letter: ARTICLES ABOUT WEMBLEY PRESENTATION	124
55. Note: RIDING THREE ALTER REAL HORSES	126
56. Letter	129
57. Note	131
58. Letter: *FLORIDO'S* EXCITEMENT	135
59. Note: NUNO RIDING MY HORSES	136
60. Letter	137
61. Note: THE MASTER WORKS WITH *CORIOLANO*	138
62. Letter: NUNO'S REFLECTIONS	138
63. Letter	140
64. Note: LETTER FROM JEAN-CLAUDE MENUT	142
65. Note: WORK IN HAND, REMARKS	143
66. Letter: TONGUE CONCERNS	144
67. Note: PIAFFE IN HAND AND MOUNTED	145
68. Note: THE MASTER RIDES TWO STUDENT HORSES	147
69. Letter: CORRECTING A LATERALIZED WALK	149
70. Letter: NEW YEAR WISHES	151
GLOSSARY	152
71. About This book	154

INTRODUCTION TO THE ENGLISH EDITION

This project was made possible by the generous help of several individuals. Without their considerable effort we would not be reading this great work in English. Mrs. Hilda Nelson spearheaded the translation process over ten years ago and brought this manuscript to our attention along with the unique collection of Mr. Henriquet's personal photographs of Nuno Oliveira and his horses. Some photos have never been published before and are not in the original French edition. We hope you enjoy the thousands of unwritten words represented by the fifty pictures presented herein. Thanks to Cavalcade, the French publisher for graciously endorsing the English edition.

A special thanks is owed to Michel Henriquet for generously sharing with us the 30 years of private correspondence and personal notes taken during his long period of study with Master Nuno Oliveira. A rare window into the insights and methods of this 20th century master is chronicled in Mr. Henriquet's unique work.

We are thankful to Jessie van Eck for reviewing the translation and verifying it with Mr. Henriquet. She added the unique benefit of ensuring that Mr. Henriquet's intent was carried through to the English reader.

Finally we are so grateful to Master Nuno Oliveira whose rare talent is pictured and chronicled here. We can only benefit from his generosity of spirit in relaying his genius to Mr. Henriquet over the course of their student—mentor relationship. Nuno Oliveira's work lives on in the work and artistry of his equestrian disciples and in the printed word. This is a testament to what was learned by one and now, shared with all.

—Richard F. Williams, Xenophon Press

TRANSLATOR'S NOTE:
At times I have given an English equivalent to some of the French expressions, while on other occasions I exclusively used the French term (example: *ramener, rassembler.*)

La Mise en main - in hand; bringing the horse in the hand; yielding of the jaw in the position of the *ramener*, on the bit.

Le Ramener - flexing of the poll, with the forehead vertical; entails a degree of collection.

La Descente de main - yielding of the hand, finger and/or rein pressure the horse must not change his pace or position; he is in self-carriage.

La Descente de jambes - yielding of legs; ceasing the action of legs.

L'effet d'ensemble - Combined or coordinated effect; use of the leg and/or spur simultaneously combined with the use of the hand.

Rassembler, rassemblé - I have used the French term *rassembler* exclusively because the English term *collection* is not quite as accurate, with a more limiting meaning. *Rassembler* describes the bearing of the horse's head in the position of the *ramener* and the hindquarters engaged in collection. When using the term *rassembler*, while *collection* is involved, it includes each and every part and action of the horse, the suppleness of his body, his back, legs, the pliancy of his *ressorts* (that is, "springs," his joints and muscles, etc.) his ease, harmony, and generosity when moving, the cadence and rhythm of his gaits, and, above all, his lightness. *Rassembler* implies the collection, the gathering together of the entire horse, the convergence of the horse's forehand and his hindquarters. It is the all-round perfection of a well schooled horse, which, together with lightness, is the crowning glory of a trainer's efforts.

Dressage - Used only to indicate the discipline (schooling of horses and competitive dressage); the English term "schooling" has been used when the actual training of horses is involved.

PREFACE

My friend, Michel Henriquet, has asked me to write a preface as part of the collection that he is publishing: namely, his correspondence with Nuno Oliveira. While the invitation is flattering and friendly, I nonetheless hesitated for some time. What could I possibly say that is new with respect to Nuno Oliveira and his art?

Jaime Celestino Da Costa and Nuno Oliveira

To convince me, Michel gave me some of his reasons and hopes. The reasons: "because you are the only witness to what was once the *manège* and teachings of Master Miranda before and after Nuno made the scene." His hopes: "in that you played a part in these undertakings and in Nuno's evolution, you ought to say a few words. That is why I am convinced that it will interest everyone and why I put my trust in you."

Let us hope that I neither contradict his reasons nor disappoint his hopes. But I fear that this may be a story that is too long which could tire the reader and, at the same time, abuse the space allotted to a simple preface.

Joachim Gonçalves De Miranda (1870-1940), a man who lived from the horse and for the horse, was an unforgettable teacher and master. While more than fifty years have passed, he continues to live in my memory in his double role: as professor of equitation and as a master and teacher of dressage [the art of schooling of horses.] These roles must be considered separately in their own right.

PROFESSOR OF EQUITATION

Monsieur Miranda, as everyone called him, (the term *maître* was seldom used), founded, at the turn of the century, a remarkable School of Equitation *("O Picadeiro do Senhor Miranda")* at number 135 on the Rua do Borja. This school was the most famous and respected in Lisbon, as well as the most frequented. Everyone, especially those belonging to elegant society, frequented Miranda's place to learn how to ride. This was, at the time, part of a person's education. Above all, young girls were able to find in this *manège* a respectable place to which they were allowed to go (accompanied by their mothers!) Thus a large number of Miranda's pupils were ladies riding side-saddle.

The School at Rua do Borja was part of Lisbon's social life. On certain afternoons, the gallery of the *manège* became the meeting point for elegant society.

As professor of equitation, Miranda was primarily concerned with preparing his pupils to be able to sit properly on a horse. He made us sit on a horse without stirrups for a whole year, which resulted in a good seat; all kinds of games and exercises taught the pupils how to guide and move their mounts: elaborate vaulting was another element obligatory to one's apprenticeship. But we did many other things such as jumping bareback with the saddle under one's arm. I learned to perform The Rose game in public, which was jumping with three horses (mounted on one horse, another led in tandem, a third close by, led only with a single halter.) Yet another feat: he presented a dozen side-saddle riders jumping simultaneously in a single row. I cannot remember having seen this accomplished elsewhere.

Miranda made us jump and participate in various horse shows. Yet this was not his forte. He did this only to give us a wide preparation for our equestrian education and to instill in us the spirit of competition. Only the most interested and gifted among his many pupils took the path of dressage - which belonged to the "upper level course" of horsemanship.

Monsieur Miranda spent the whole day in the *manège*, never frequented any non-equestrian entertainment and never lunched nor dined in town. He drank only cold tea (never alcohol) and

Master MIRANDA, 1913.

smoked cigarettes which he rolled himself.

When he moved about in Lisbon he went either on horseback or used a little one-horse American phaeton to go to the boot maker (Barroso, *père*), the saddle maker, or to visit his friends (Monsieur Chatelanaz, his friend and "sponsor," as we would say today.) I often accompanied him and he allowed me to drive. Just before his death, he was preparing a certificate on my behalf which would have allowed me to have a license as coachman. I still regret never getting it.

Life in Lisbon during the thirties was peaceful. Monsieur Miranda worked in his *manège* until the day of his death which occurred just after he returned home from a ride on his horse.

MIRANDA, Dressage Master

As *écuyer* in the Royal House, Miranda could have been influenced by a pupil of Baucher, namely Brunot, and General Vito Moreira who had worked in Saumur for three years. Not much is known about the equestrian youth of Miranda. He, himself, did not often speak about this period.

He claimed to be a "Fillist" (as it was fashionable in Portugal), but comparing the text and the photos of Fillis with the dressage of Miranda, one becomes aware that they have nothing in common.

My Master was an instinctive artist, undoubtedly self-educated, an *écuyer* belonging to the national tradition (as are those horsemen practicing bullfighting and other isolated disciplines of the equestrian art.) We would have known a little more about the influences he received if a large framed board in the shape of a horseshoe which featured in the gallery of the *manège* and filled with photographs had not disappeared. It entailed this caption: "*Écuyers* whom Miranda had known and admired." I retain only two pictures in my memory: that of D. José Manuel da Cunha Meneses (Sr.) executing a brilliant passage; and that of Captain Caeiro, executing a magnificent Spanish trot.

Having lived so many years close to Master Miranda, seeing him ride and teach, I, who was taught by him and received his advice, became convinced that he lived primarily through his equestrian genius and by an art based on experience, acquired in the course of his long life.

Miranda followed no "method." Neither did he follow any classical books on equitation which, I believe, he did not know and, certainly, did not possess. He "read" horses, not books.

He did not travel and was not personally acquainted with the great foreign masters, his contemporaries. Furthermore, living in a town that was, at the time, not very cosmopolitan, one can state that Miranda's art was his own.

Still young, he had presented himself, with great success, at two public dressage events. In the first one, he won the First Prize on a horse of Alter lineage (*Favorito*.) In the second event he presented three Thoroughbred horses (from the stud of Conde de Sobral) and won three first prizes. With the first prize on Dartmoor he executed,

The student *amazones* of Master MIRANDA

amongst other airs, 150 lead changes at every canter stride (with voltes and rein changes.) When he was through facing the Jury, the three judges got up with a single bound, hat in hand.

It was Miranda himself who told me this and which helped him devote his life as a dressage teacher.

Miranda was a very simple man, friendly (despite terrible but fleeting rages), modest, yet aware of his value. He could have answered in the same manner as did Jules Renard, author of "*Histoires Naturelles*" who, when asked what his conception of himself was, answered, "it is bad when I look at myself, but much better when I compare myself to others."

Monsieur Miranda dressed very simply when riding: long trousers of the same material as the jacket (a real suit) or a black blazer, rubber ankle boots and box spurs with delicate rowels. No gloves.

One had the impression that he wanted to be as close to the horse as possible (hands and legs) and that his dress was not an important aspect of his art. Mounted, Miranda was totally relaxed. Slightly bent forwards in the last years of his life, he had a perfect seat as though glued to the saddle.

He never tried to appear handsome on his horse, to *show* himself; rather, he wanted to *show off his horse*, give him the best appearance. Having extraordinary "feeling" for the horse, as soon as he was mounted, regardless of the kind of horse he was on or the level of his schooling, he transformed the horse immediately. Miranda gave him correct carriage, putting him at the *rassembler* and collected him. One would think he was on a different horse. And he, the master, was not aware of the little marvel that he had created. To him, this was simply as it should be!

With Miranda one held the reins only in the left hand, those of the curb bit adjusted, those of the snaffle bit above, either falling in loops or more adjusted. Acting with the right hand on the right rein of the snaffle. This classical way of holding the reins was usual to us, being prescribed by the practice of bullfighting and side-saddle riding. It must not be forgotten. One used both hands to hold the reins only in the breaking of the horse and for sports equitation. When schooling, the curb bit was added on early to the snaffle after the horse was started. A gentle S-bit was used with delicacy when dealing with a quiet, but relaxed mouth, achieved by means of flexions performed in hand.

The position was somewhat low, with the horse's back never hollow, one of the factors leading to a perfectly immobile head, fixed, but without any contraction [rigidity] in the neck. The tail fell motionless. There was never any tail-lashing provoked by the spur. One had the image of a calm horse, and calmness reigned on horseback.

Miranda followed the formula "hands like silk and legs of cotton wool" and exhibited perfect accord between hands and legs.

His hands gave the appearance of immobility by their fixity, while there was great mobility and lightness in the fingers, sometimes in the wrists.

But the secret of my Master could be found in the way he used his legs: his long trousers, rubber ankle boots and box spurs, set quite low, gave him considerable freedom to adjust his legs to the horse, enveloping and caressing its skin, but without being clamped, always ready to produce a well-placed stroke, mobilizing the foot, lowering the toe and raising the heel.

Master Miranda rigorously followed the advice of Fillis "for the true *écuyers*, the use of legs; for the ineffective ones, the whip." Thus the whip was not used in mounted dressage. If when mounted, one needed to correct certain airs or exercises, this was done with the help of the legs (together with hands and seat) and not by means of a whip. This was one of the most personal traits of the *maître*'s type of dressage.

Should one wish to describe this kind of dressage in one word, one must say that the horses were extremely well-schooled. At no time were they robots merely prepared to execute fixed programs; rather, they were so prepared to respond to the aids at any time and to change or alternate the exercises.

The important foundations of dressage were total lightness, a *rassemblé* adapted to the exercise, and a permanent impulsion at the walk, trot, and canter, with perfect cadence and the horse very straight. **The secret of great artists is to perfectly execute the simple things.**

The walk, halt, departure, and correct rein back were the other requirements of his work.

Joachim Goncalves de MIRANDA riding Favorito, passage

There was no extended trot required, only ample trots. One did not execute the shoulder-in, for that did not exist [in his method.] One did not work at the pillars, nor did one execute the high airs.

The half-passes were less bent than they are today, but horses never plunged forward [losing their balance.] Minor tricks such as oscillating the shoulders or pirouettes on three legs were regarded as a game of no importance.

However, certain difficult airs such as the backwards canter could be executed to perfection. The horse *Azeitona* is the only one I have seen who could execute a backwards canter with four tempi changes with gliding transitions from canter in place, to canter backwards, and back to canter in place. This was the result of a regulated *rassemblé* and permanent impulsion. The same horse executed very straight lead changes at tempo, in all directions as well as the series 6, 5, 4, 3, 2, 1, 2, 3, 4, 5, 6 without missing a single one. *Azeitona* was my "schoolmaster" when it came to suppleness, equilibrium, impulsion, and perfection.

Nevertheless, the passage was the most impressive of the school airs that Monsieur Miranda executed. Even to this day one speaks of *"a passage à la Miranda."* As far as I am concerned, the secret came from the action of his legs, relaxed but not loose, acting with the precision of a stopwatch, using diagonal aids, placed far back, which "animated" each and every stride with great subtlety, even when dealing with already well-schooled horses. We will come back to this later.

What did Nuno Oliveira see or learn in the school of Maître Miranda, and what was his subsequent evolution?

This question is not easy to answer. I can only speak of Nuno's background. He and I were born in the same neighborhood of Lisbon, 200 meters away from each other ten years apart. I still live there.

Nuno's father, Guido Oliveira, a Protestant pastor, was a quiet and affable man, who rode at his cousin's place, Monsieur Miranda, where he took his eleven year old son in 1936. I had been riding there [at Miranda's] *since* 1924. When Nuno arrived, I had been already riding less often, immersed in my medical studies. At that time, I was perhaps, despite my absences, the most advanced pupil of the school.

These circumstances led the young beginner Nuno to judge me as a great horseman. Error in diagnosis! I remember the appearance of the young man as he was then: dark, slender, nervous, and enthusiastic who, it seemed to me, was not greatly attuned to equitation. Error in prognosis!

But on the occasion of the death and funeral of Miranda in 1940, Nuno, aged fifteen, allowed us to guess the kind of person he would become some years later.

Together with a great number of pupils and friends, we followed on foot, through the streets of Lisbon, the hearse pulled by a sad-looking horse. The passers-by stopped, astonished by this anachronistic and unusual funeral procession.

At the cemetery a strange event disturbed the solemnity of the moment. When the coffin was being lowered down into the earth, Nuno rushed forward with violence and attempted to prevent its lowering, not wanting to be separated from his master. We had to remove him from the spot by force. A minor scandal.

Nuno, the unpredictable and passionate one, had revealed himself.

With the death of Miranda, having neither descendants nor associates, the school closed, to the great sorrow of the pupils.
I stopped riding and lost sight of Nuno.

I saw him on horseback again only in 1944. At that time, looking at him, one thought of a rider of Golega: thin, very straight, rigid, reins held too long, hands held close to his stomach. He reminded one of Don Quixote. It was his crossing of the desert. People considered him (according to what I have been told) to be somewhat of an eccentric.

I found Nuno once again in February 1962. He had invited me several times to visit him. Having finished my competitive examination for a professorship an the Department of Surgery, I decided to visit him at his school in Povoa de Santo Adriao which was unfamiliar to me.

He was mad with joy. With his typical urgency, he lent me trousers and ankle boots and made me, that same day, after twenty years of equestrian fasting, get on three of his dressage horses

Nuno Oliveira in 1944

(*Saturno, Beaugeste,* and *Tesouro.*)

I could no longer help myself. The young man I had known as a beginner, uncertain of his career, had now become an accomplished master. I became his pupil.

But he never wanted to explicitly recognize the new situation: the "junior" who had now become the master, and the "elder," the pupil. Until the end, he retained a respectful attitude towards me with one exception! He never once in his writings, referred to me as one of his pupils, which would have honored me greatly, me, the simple amateur of equestrian art, embarrassed at having to hold four reins in two hands and handle a whip.

In this year 1962 I discovered a new equestrian world. Nuno Oliveira was at his peak. He had already become familiar with the

Nuno Oliveira, around 1944

Vienna School and Podhajsky in Lisbon (1954.) He had become familiar with Manuel Barros and his important equestrian library; and had already schooled his first significant group of horses at Azeitao.

The names of La Guérinière, Baucher, Beudant, d'Aure, L'Hotte, Faverot de Kerbrech, Raabe, Decarpentry, and others had become familiar names at the school at Povoa where one could find pupils of great quality such as Diogo Lafoes, Guilherme Borba, and Pureza Sao Louranço.

Baumeister had invited him and organized a presentation in Geneva in 1960, and the first French horsemen (Persin, Henriquet, and Bacharach)came to see him.

In short, he was going to launch an international career on all six continents. It is the story of a well-known success which I will not retell.

Thus, when I renewed my contact with equitation, a great distance in time, milieu and work-methods had developed between Miranda and Nuno Oliveira -- a real gulf. Once again, I saw Lisbon and was reminded of Miranda's provincial life when the young Nuno Oliveira frequented the *manège* in Rua do Borja and the conditions he had found there: a *maître* of a certain age, a limited equitation program, but of outstanding quality, an absence of books on equitation and no real equestrian culture, limited discussions pertaining to dressage methods, and no outside contact. Furthermore, a professor with too many pupils, undifferentiated, who took up almost his entire day, but whom he needed in order to live. A master with a limited number of school horses for which he could not pay out of his own pocket.

On the other hand, I had before me a young teacher with already considerable experience based on the theories of equestrian art and a great variety of means which resulted in a superior practice of *haute école* and new procedures. All of this occurred in an international ambience, using a multitude of horses which came to him from all directions and which passed under his saddle.

How did Nuno regard Maître Miranda and what did he think of the actual influence he had on him?

Let us listen to him talking about his teacher: "The concept of the role of *Écuyer* and the immense talent with which he filled this role, has given me forever the cult of this profession." And further on: "With respect to the Equitation of the *Maître*, I perfectly remember his tremendous discipline, the calmness of his horses,d their perfect submission and his insistence on obtaining halts from which all his horses could execute any *haute école* air. The canter had an extraordinary fluidity, lead changes were extremely brilliant, very ample, and the passage was executed with the greatest moments of suspension I have ever seen."

Despite his youth and inexperience during the period when he was Miranda's pupil, one senses that the latter had sent Nuno a real message. He was too young to form a complete analysis of his teacher's art. Yet, re-reading Nuno's writing, I realized that something more had been retained in his mind, and that this formidable personal experience had not been erased.

I choose an example which seems to me paradigmatic. In a short chapter written by Nuno in one of his books on the use of the legs, he tells us what we have to do. "Much has been written about a rider's hands, but there are few equitation treatises that deal with the problem of the legs... one tends to abuse leg pressure.... The legs must be lowered, close to the horse, but gentle, immobile, and they must touch quickly, yield, touch again, yield again in a fraction of a second. Almost all of the riders I have seen have their legs glued to the horse, the heel always impeccably lowered, the spurs usually placed very high, but unaware whether they are touching or not. When the spur is placed too high, certain subtle touches are not possible and one has to place the toe down to obtain a supple heel... the elegance in the use of the spur as a means of suppling only occurs with few *écuyers*... but as an aid to achieve suppleness, spurs with a rowel are more precise and more subtle."

What Nuno actually wants to describe is the use of his own legs. Nowhere in his accounts, be it a quote from a treatise or a reference to another horseman, does this idea exist.

However, what he does achieve with excellence, is a detailed and correct description of *Maître* Miranda's leg actions, which I had witnessed throughout all these years.

Lacking a film or video which did not exist at the time, a photo of Miranda on *Favorito* (around 1911) sufficiently demonstrates this. This horse is executing a brilliant passage, the left diagonal is in the air, with Miranda, quietly and correctly seated, showing us his legs lowered but not glued to the horse. He wears long trousers, rubber ankle boots, and his box spurs with rowels, placed naturally and very low. But if one looks under the horse's belly on the other side, one can clearly see the lowered tip of the right foot, which obviously corresponds to the raising of the right heel and right spur subtly touching the horse's sides at the exact moment the opposite diagonal is elevated. The opposite will occur at the next stride when the right diagonal is raise,: the tip of the left foot will be lowered and the spur will delicately touch the horse. Why delicately? Because everything occurs in a state of calmness and immobility on the part of then rider, while only the legs act.

This photograph gives us the perfect image of what his master could do and which Nuno asks us to do, as though it were one of his own ideas. In a Freudian manner, one could say that in his subconscious, Nuno had kept memory from his youth of which he was unaware.

Other comparisons could be made if I had the time, space and necessary talent to demonstrate the unsuspected influence of Miranda's equitation on that of Nuno. We often think that we are doing something new but which we have actually seen accomplished by our ancestors.

Nuno, who had become a very original *maître*, despite the new elements in his art and the richness of his experience, was the only horseman who, in his posture and that of his horses, reminded me of my master and his distinctive equitation. I insist that something did remain in the memory of Nuno Oliveira with respect to his childhood experience with Miranda. *The means* had certainly changed but the results resembled each other.

Equitation, like so many other human activities, has certain *archetypes* which are passed from one period to another, one system to another, one individual to another. They represent a *continuity* that innovators, no matter how brilliant, cannot erase.

—Jaime Celestino da Costa

Professor Jaime da Costa - Hioral, Alter Real, 1975

Nuno Oliveira with *Beau Geste* in pesade

"Henriquet,
In memory of my trip to Paris where you very kindly received me.
- Nuno"

INTRODUCTION

At the end of many years devoted to a careful and extensive study of equitation and the *Baucherist* experience under the learned authority of René Bacharach, many questions arose which seemed unanswerable to me.

Bacharach, the last supporter of this somewhat cursed methodology, shared with me this dissatisfaction, but justified it by blaming its weaknesses on the poor interpretations of texts. In 1946 and 1947, he met several times Captain Étienne Beudant, already old and ill. The latter died in 1949. Bacharach pledged a profound admiration to this talented self-educated rider, an admirer of General Faverot de Kerbrech [*Methodical Dressage of the Riding Horse*, Xenophon Press 2010.]

Generals de Kerbrech and L'Hotte were the two preferred disciples of François Baucher. I was very lucky to benefit from the lights of such a direct affiliation, even if I was accumulating certain doubts along practical and intellectual lines.

Beudant was a simple, intelligent and subtle man. He was a junior officer who did not go through military school. Still, he had daily contact with the prestigious Faverot who, in 1903, was his colonel in the 23rd Dragoons. The official and social difference, separating the two officers of such diverse social classes, was relatively impassable at the time.

René Bacharach told me that Beudant had never worked with Faverot. He had exchanged some thoughts and at least corresponded with him. He had admitted to Bacharach that he had been able to observe Faverot on horseback "only though the peephole of the *Manège* door."

This had sufficed to prompt the captain's interest in the work of his colonel, namely, *"Dressage Methodique du Cheval de Selle"* [*Methodical Dressage of the Riding Horse,* Faverot de Kerbrech, Xenophon Press 2010], and since this work had become unavailable, Beudant, in 1923, published a *résumé* entitled *"Extérieur et Haute École,"* [*Horse Training: Outdoors and High School,* Xenophon Press 2014] which he then completed in 1938 with his *"Dressage du Cheval de Selle."*

It was around 1958, that, with all the affection and respect I had for René Bacharach, I could no longer delay admitting to him that we had reached a dead-end, that our dressage no longer progressed and that it would be best to reconsider the problem.

With his characteristic honesty, he put me in contact with Colonel Bouhet, General de Champvallier and General Gassiat, all *Baucherists*, all having briefly been Beudant's pupils, verbally, for at the time Beudant was already disabled.

I found in their horsemanship the same disarray, despite the fact that they had practical experience for more than ten years and a complete equestrian background, extending to all the authors and teachers of the school of Baucher.

It was these men who urged me to pursue my quest towards the south Iberian peninsula where they had observed among certain bullfighters, horses with astounding *equilibrium*, similar to that which we were seeking. According to them, this balance had been obtained through the exceptional conformation and temperament of their horses rather than from their skill or method, which, after all, was rather brutal.

I was coming from Lisbon when, one fine day in 1959, I received the man who was to transform not only my equestrian life, but my life itself, namely, *Maître* Oliveira.

I received him at my place, surrounded by my friends, when he left Portugal for the first time on his way to Geneva to present a horse he had sold.

However, he had a few photographs in his pocket and an eight mm film. Contemplating all this instilled in us great admiration. We had before us an animated image conforming to the engravings of La Guérinière with respect to the horse's brilliance and his equilibrium.

The questions that followed testified to his perfect knowledge of French and foreign classical authors. He ignored neither the works nor the philosophy of Solomon de la Broue up to the least important disciples of Baucher, as well as the German classics such as Steinbrecht to the early Italian masters.

Pressed by General de Champvallier as well as René Bacharach to admit that he was a Baucherist, a supporter of work in place as well as neck elevation. This he did straightforwardly, all the while evoking several times the *écuyers* who belonged to the *Grande*

Écurie of Versailles.

I brought him my two Thoroughbreds with great embarrassment. He mounted them and we discovered two different horses possessing a beautiful balance and cadence unknown to us. Twenty years later, he confided to me with humor, "You know, I was very intimidated at having met French horsemen, heirs of La Guérinière and pupils of Baucher, but, ultimately you were... quite sympathetic."

A few weeks later, he greeted me at the Lisbon airport through the V.I.P. exit, and I was his guest for eight days. He initiated me into an intense program which began at six in the morning and ended at eight at night.

The honor he gave me compared sharply with the distant attitude he often had with important persons who came from all over the world. I was the first foreign apprentice to visit him. I belonged to the nation which, to him, was the cradle of "his" equitation. He would never admit that one could speak of a Portuguese equitation, even less of an *Oliveiriste* one.

His attitude towards today's great equestrian practices seemed to me somewhat ambiguous at that time. Actually, he feared offending those convictions which, he believed, all French horsemen held deeply.

It was only after a true relationship between master and disciple had established itself that I began to understand the philosophical and theoretical choices he had made, taken from among the best and fullest to be found in the *École de Versailles*, which had come to an end with the eighteenth century, and from the Baucherist school which had appeared out of nowhere during the first half of the following century.

Whereas here with us, from 1833 to the present, our *écuyers* adopted or rejected Baucherist propositions without distinction, equestrian Europe, after a brief period of curiosity, held them up to public criticism. Yet, there existed a young *écuyer*, who, day after day, with passionate fury, took apart the best that could be found among the many doctrines, and then in the remote distances of Iberia brought together an invaluable French equitation.

The acculturation [process of intercultural borrowing] which set upon the equestrian world of France since the end of the nineteenth century only led to petty quarrels and its ultimate disappearance, whereas our neighbors from the east, after having duly eliminated Baucher as the "grave-digger of French equitation," evolved towards draw-reins, compression, and the institutionalization of the *"trot plané"* [a poorly performed, perverted, passage trot, a term used by Gustav Steinbrecht] all in the name of La Guérinière.

At the time of our encounter, the *maître*'s life was still relatively peaceful. On horseback from around six in the morning, he worked colts and young horses alone in the early morning, then gave a lesson to one of his paying guests. After lunch he wrote a little, gave lessons to the children from a boarding school, rode his most advanced horse, and then gave further lessons until 8:30 in the evening. His clients were essentially Portuguese, apart from a few foreigners residing in Lisbon.

In the evening, when horse-breeders and bullfighters, who had entrusted their horses to him for training (or retraining!), returned from their farms, they stopped at the *"Picadeiro"* of the master to observe his work or to chat with him at the fireplace which was at the farthest end of the gallery.

The equestrian background of many of these country horsemen was extensive and extended to all the European teachers. They held passionate discussions on the merits of various horses and on the concepts of the various Schools, from those of Versailles, of Baucher, to the principles of the "most excellent Marquis de Marialva."

I listened with fascination to these horsemen born in and from another age. It was the Great Nuncio, breeder, agriculturist, but above all, the first and foremost bullfighter of all times, who gave me, on horses trained for bullfighting, the notion of a canter pirouette when facing an adversary.

There were also the fabulous breeders such as Andrade. I have come to know four generations of them, all great horsemen, the brothers Carlos and Manuel Veiga, the Palhas, and many others less known but also interesting.

Among the foreigners who had discovered where they could find the equestrian talent in Lisbon were the French and Swiss ambassadors, andMadame Counselor of the Embassy of the Netherlands. Today I am reading an interview with Princess Dona

Pilar de Bourbon, sister of the King of Spain, currently president of the FEI who speaks of her youth in exile in Portugal with her brothers: "They sent us to a little *manège* with a magnificent professor." In 1960 she was a discrete and charming co-disciple.

Whenever an important international bull fighting event took place in the Lisbon arenas, the great masters of this martial art never failed to pay a visit to Nuno when he was working his horses.

Contact with father and son Domecq, the brothers Peralta, the Bohorques and their *"quadrilla"* [the team that accompanies a bullfighter in the ring] was marked by interest and the respectful distance one feels when meeting artists who are experts in similar yet different disciplines.

The "permanent" riders of the *manège*, despite the frictions which marked their relationship with a difficult teacher, continued to stay by his side. All horsemen noted for the subtlety of their aids, and their scientific knowledge, made their debut at his *manège* towards 1956 when he installed himself at Odivelas, a suburb of Lisbon, in a site that belonged to Monsieur Julio Borba.

The first person I met was Doctor Guilherme Borba who was completing his veterinary studies and was taking a daily lesson at noon, until, twenty years later; he undertook the creation and direction of *l'École Portugaise Nationale d'Art Equestre* [Portuguese School of Equestrian Art.]

The very distinguished professor Jaime da Costa who, prior to Nuno Oliveira, was a pupil of Master Miranda: a great surgeon, an outstanding *écuyer*, humanist and wonderful friend.

Don José Athayde, who also carries the heritage of the *maître*, Dom Diogo de Bragança, [*Dressage in the French Tradition*, Xenophon Press 2011] whose equitation is a convergence of classical equestrian background mixed with his own humorous personality and elegant fantasy.

The youngest among us and without doubt the last authentic disciple of the master: Joao Trigueiros de Aragao, a rider who perfectly represents our ideal of subtlety and brilliance.

At that time Joao Oliveira was thirteen years old and the rather rough equestrian relationship he had with his father kept him away from the *manège*. It is at my place that he resumed his link with equitation by giving his first lessons to one of my friends.

Don Jose Athayde, student of Nuno Oliveira

Joao used the money to buy himself a pair of jeans.

All these individuals who are very dear friends were also friends of Master Oliveira. They accompanied him during his most active thirty years of equestrian life and are present in these notes and correspondence.

The equitation as it was practiced among us was more a common quest rather than rivalry, and I believe, was part of our life and an element of joy, very far removed from the state of mind found among high caliber competitive horsemen. These fraternal relationships, involving one of the most complex arts, continue to survive.

When I began this long road under the direction of the master, I owned an English Thoroughbred stallion and mare. That same year I discovered the very horse unknown to the rest of Europe and totally forgotten then called the Andalusian pure-bred.

During my first visit, I bought one of them named *Andaluz* that Nuno had already started under saddle a few weeks prior and sent him to me with precious recommendations.

**Dom Diogo de Bragança, student of Nuno Oliveira,
author of *Dressage in the French Traditon*, Xenophon Press**

Although during these thirty years I never spent more than three months without seeing him either at his place or mine, *Andaluz* and my Thoroughbreds were the first subjects of a friendly and technical correspondence of which I am presenting only the parts pertaining to equitation. These epistolary exchanges were a rare privilege over fifteen years. Later, his daughter Pureza ran his secretarial office and my questions, without being exhausted, became less frequent and mostly on the telephone.

At the start of my four yearly periods as a trainee, I kept a thick notebook where I pointed out in a shorthand but precise manner everything that I discovered and ascertained as I observed him working. Later, I continued to take notes when I rode under his tutelage.

I was given another tremendous privilege, namely, that he had me ride only his personal horses.

Nothing pertaining to my aptitude or results justified such a favor, except perhaps my immense curiosity and the admiration that I immediately had for him which I showed by my incessant and sometimes undoubtedly importunate questions.

Belonging to a country, France, where dressage had almost reached an abyss but where the mind was sharpened through years of discussions, disappointing yet at times exhilarating studies, our conversations were occasionally ablaze with passion.

He felt my amazement as I observed him, studied him, and, at the same time, he discerned in some of my remarks, reservations which disturbed him. For I was marked by this sort of Puritanism which characterizes *Baucherists,* this rejection by my first initiators of all means other than those belonging to the *Maître du Cirque des Champs Elysées* [Riding Master of the Circus of the Champs Elysées, a reference to Baucher.]

I progressively noticed the wealth of sources and means that Nuno Oliveira put into his work which did not always follow *Baucherist* orthodoxy. Here and there appeared elements in the purest Versailles tradition. The shoulder-in was, indeed, the basis of all his work and I saw that he was not very interested in raising the neck via the hand but, rather, by flexing all the joints through lateral movements and by riding transitions with a lot of impulsion.

He most often made references to the famous German *écuyer* of the nineteenth century, Gustav Steinbrecht, [*Gymnasium of the Horse,* Xenophon Press 2011] and had lent me a translated copy, since the translation by Commandant Dupont had not yet been published. In this work I found many of the principles and procedures Nuno used in his work. Steinbrecht represented the German school in the nineteenth century, indefectibly faithful to the School of Versailles, and stigmatized Baucher as a corruptor of the equestrian art.

It was only after working with him year after year that I became more and more aware of the choices and evolutions of the master which enabled him to achieve the goal he had set for himself and to which he will return constantly in his correspondence: the *balance (equilibrium) and lightness through impulsion in the cadence, the basic measure of rhythm.*

Based on the equestrian foundation perfectly defined by La Guérinière, Oliveira never ceased to dip into the technology put at his disposal by French classical and foreign authors which his tremendous background made possible.

He was a *Baucherist* as far as yielding of the aids was concerned, alternating hand and leg, the breaking down of resistances through halts, transitions, and flexions with stiff horses. But he always returned to Versailles and the *"École de Cavalerie"*, [*École de Cavalerie Part II (School of Horsemanship)*, Xenophon Press 1992] the monument of world equestrian literature, for everything that dealt with the artistic and poetic aspect of equitation, and, above all, the *rassembler.*

When considering equilibrium, he always gave preference to the suppling and flexion of the haunches in their forward movement. He definitely refuted the direct raising of the neck in place by the hand which had been the trap, "the pit" into which so many *Baucherists* fell.

An anecdote illustrates his attitudes towards what is, nonetheless, an essential part of *Baucherism.* I was watching him work a Luso-English horse with a hollow back. He strained his wits to lower the neck and to by put the horse in suspension, on circles, at the shoulder-in. Then dismounting, he takes three works by Beudant, spreads them on a bench in the gallery and asks me, "What inspiration do these photographs give you with their excessive raising of the neck and, yet, showing a certain quality in the execution of the airs?" Then, answering his own question, he said: "If you have read Beudant carefully, remember that as an officer of native affairs in Morocco, he moved about continually with his horses and worked them between two villages. Thereby he escaped, only partly, the damage done by schooling in place which did so much damage to the *Baucherists*."

The tremendous merit of Nuno Oliveira, which, had he not appeared on the international equestrian scene at a time of complete lack of culture, would have brought him glory, is that he achieved *in vivo* this synthesis of two complementary techniques, two similar philosophies which emerged from different concepts.

The intellectual poverty of the modern world of horsemanship was able to draw from it only that which divided it and made it sterile.

When watching the master, one could see the engravings of Parrocel [Charles, engraver, 1688-1752] come to life. One took part in his work, and heard him proclaim the importance of the trot and its indispensable tonicity. One admired his work at the measured and collected walk, the lowering of the haunches through halts and half-halts, the sumptuous shoulder-in, croup to the wall, his obsession with lightness and brilliance. But one came upon Baucher when the master "broke down force and movement" to make contractions dissolve with "hand without legs; legs without hand," when working in hand, when yielding with the hand, when commencing "application of the spur," and the "combined effect" [*effet d'ensemble.*]

With this double inspiration, which no author nor French *écuyer* had unreservedly adopted, he explicitly fused a single body of doctrine. This gave us those perfect *rassemblers* of Master Oliveira.

Using the right keys with the two methods explains the extraordinary cadences of his horses, their musical rhythm, which never ceased to preoccupy him, as did lightness and equilibrium, which are their components.

He was perfectly aware of his use of the methods and principles of the ancient masters and never failed to stress the origins of a particular movement which allowed him to succeed. He never felt the need to dwell upon his sources of inspiration and the importance of taking components from one or the other school.

Since Oliveira's departure I have noted in the international press that some placed upon him the label of a pure and uncompromising *Baucherist* and at times I found myself involved as witness in these technical, literary disputes. The publication of this correspondence, wherein the master expresses himself quite freely and without being preoccupied with an audience, will put matters into perspective. When we lost him in 1989, I decided to send to Branca Oliveira and her children photocopies of these letters. They are still in her hands.

During our epistolary exchange, I only kept those portions which were strictly devoted to equitation, which explains an absence of dates, since I did not always keep the first page and the master did not always systematically date his letters.

Readers who did not know him will perhaps be surprised by his explanations in the form of justifications pertaining to his public equestrian appearances. Except for one case where I found a second copy of one of my letters, I did not preserve my own correspondence, which may render somewhat obscure certain arguments in which he defends one or the other of his public presentations or his dressage.

One tragic thing that occurred in his life was that he was never able to train a horse worthy of his abilities. First, it was a question of not having the necessary finances. He always bought directly from lesser known breeders, thus the least expensive, somewhat mediocre horses. When he approached the best-known breeders, he usually took from them their second best, almost handicapped horses.

The evolution, then the transformation of these creatures was spectacular, especially when one considered what they were initially. It was legitimate to go into rapture, which we never failed to do. Nonetheless, one never changes a duck into a swan and we were frustrated never to see this immense talent working with something worthy of him.

When some friends were involved in competitions, we become aware of his tremendous qualities in the international press, and soon presentations were organized in the principal cities of Europe, South America, and the U.S.A. To acknowledge them he used the horses he had, even those he did not have, or those he had trained and sold to amateurs who, at times, betrayed him by not having ridden them for over two years; thus he was able to rehearse with them only once before a performance!

Later, thanks to the admiration that moneyed foreign pupils had for him, he was several times offered horses of great quality. He refused to accept them in no uncertain terms. One of his most enthusiastic pupils asked me one day to select two horses of superior quality regardless of the price. I explained that we would only be rebuffed. Years later I revealed to him this scheme. He reacted by laughing and said to me "Bravo, you know me like a brother."

He certainly enjoyed solving insurmountable difficulties and to thwart the most pessimistic forecasts. We, his closest disciples, always appreciated his feats of valor at their proper worth, but we poorly hid our wish to see the virtuoso play on a Stradivarius.

The better I got to know him, the more I learned, the more I admired and was eager to see him make a successful move on the international equestrian scene. It was obvious that without a partner measuring up to him, the projected image would always be reduced.

He sensed my disappointment and took it badly, undoubtedly seeing a lack of confidence or an inability to appreciate him, which was not the case. But, alas, may have been the case with respect to those who were less informed. Some of his letters bear witness to this mixture of irritation and sadness.

One must also explain what seems to appear in other writings, namely a kind of self-satisfaction, which could shock one if taken as unbridled vanity.

Nuno Oliveira's immense passion for his art was evident, continually perceptible, throughout each moment of his life. All his gestures and thoughts converged on a single goal-to transcend today wherein he had succeeded yesterday. His relentless search for an always more delicate and refined equilibrium, each day a technique that was freer, more brilliant, went far beyond the dreams of a good *écuyer*.

This pursuit, so infinitely subtle, of an invisible communication through a permanent fusion, exalted him all the more as he succeeded more and more. Sometimes the finality of his art seemed to reside more in the excellence of his progress rather than in the realization of the actual airs.

Is it possible to distance oneself from the modern concepts of contemporary equitation in dressage where an approximate and vulgar outcome justifies the coarseness of the means?

Admiration and adhesion on the part of a few did not suffice in giving peace and quiet to what must have actually been frustration. Frustration due to being knowledgeable and not being immediately understood, followed by all, recognized as the premiere equestrian mind of his time, which he was for us, but which, for him, was insufficient. To whom better suited than him this pathetic reflection of a writer, tortured as he was, proclaiming, "To be the only one to know that you are the best is to become anyone."

This explains the inordinate behavior which was the manifestation of the discomfort of a great artist.

I have interpolated between these letters the essential part of my notes which I never ceased to make in the course of these many years. They are at times the summary of a film I saw in the *manège*. At times I call attention very carefully to some advice and reflections which have the value of precepts. Finally I note the criticisms and comments addressed to me by the *maître* in the course of a meeting when we worked together. I believe that this sum of didactic elements will remind all those who had the good fortune to work with him, of the essential aspect of his philosophy in its most direct form, and for all those who, alas, never knew this pleasure, it will add to the discovery they can make by getting to know his work.

—Michel Henriquet

Michel Henriquet and Miguelista, Lusitano, 1980

1. Letter: ADDRESSING A FRENCH DISCIPLE

The master addresses a French disciple, which is important, for to him equestrian art is French, a disciple whom he does not want to scare away, for it could imply the condemnation of certain *Baucherist* procedures. This disciple has just followed for many years the most rigorous *Baucherist* rules under the authority of the last direct heir of that school directly in line of Baucher, namely, Captain Étienne Beudant [*Horse Training: Outdoors and High School*, Xenophon Press 2014].

I found the rough draft of a letter which must have been typed by a secretary and sent as an answer to the *maître*. It is dated November 1962, a period when we still used the conventional *vous* [formal.] I will not delay disclosing the essential role of La Guérinière in the equestrian background of the *maître*. He has, as yet, not admitted it to me.

"Dear Monsieur Henriquet,

Yesterday I received a letter from your friend Persin. He tells me that he would like to come along with you.

I suggest that you work all the horses, even those I usually work alone at 5 o'clock in the morning. I believe that during the stillness of the morning you will be able to ask me questions and we will study together all the problems.

My last horse, *Altivo*, with whom I began to work after my return from Geneva, is quite outstanding. His progress is tremendous and his disposition is excellent.

When you come back you will see that I do not work my horses one hundred per cent in accordance with the second manner of Baucher.

I consider Baucher the greatest equestrian genius, and the principles of his method, the results he obtains and claims, are formidable. However, never moving away from the question of suppleness and lightness, I believe that horses, according to their conformation, their disposition, and their gaits, cannot all be trained by his method, namely, by the maximum elevation of the neck.

I claim that my horses are raised on the forehand, as you have seen, but there are some [horses that] one must not start out by elevating [the forehand.] They are the ones with necks that are thick, short, and ewe-necked, have a concave back, and weak hocks.

With them, one must wait until that elevation and perfect lightness appear as a result of an effective suppling of the back and the hind legs.

There are certain horses that I work a great deal in hand with the whip. I insist upon using a little adaptation of the work invented by [Captain] Raabe. These are the horses with very defective backs and a poor equilibrium. This type of method muscles their back, balances them, and when I work them mounted they are ready to move in top form.

I want to get on all the horses with slippers on my feet and my trousers touching [the sides of the horse] lightly and the reins held at semi-tension.

I find that you have exaggerated somewhat the elevation of the neck.

When I raise the neck and it holds itself up of its own accord, I let the head fall [stop supporting] immediately. An excessive and lengthy elevation can result in weak loins, tired hind legs, and prevent the engagement of the haunches.

I am not against elevation of the neck, but in equitation one must not exaggerate anything.

With your passion for equitation and your taste, I am very happy to have the opportunity to discuss and study with you some of these problems.

I want horses to have great impulsion and fire, but be lead with a silk thread. They must be on the go, brilliant, mobile. I cannot stand working under conditions of restraint, flaccidly, and lifelessness.

Here are four photographs of my work, they are not perfect, but they demonstrate my desire for lightness.

Receive, dear Monsieur Henriquet, my best sentiments."

Here is my answer:

"Dear *Maître*,

A thousand thanks for your letter. They herald, at least for me, a passionate exchange. What an exalted program you announce to me!

31

I understood quite well that you do not feel obligated to practice 100% the second manner [of Baucher.] Let us be precise: the one reported by Faverot [*Methodical Dressage of the Riding Horse* by Faverot de Kerbrech, Xenophon Press 2010.] Despite this, you obtain lightness which is the justification of *haute école*.

Furthermore, although my *forté* is more theoretical than practical, I am very interested in what you call "the interpretations" you give to the method of Baucher and would like to know and understand what you mean.

Your observations with respect to the extreme elevation of the neck are quite logical. Do you regard it as an error of the *Méthode* [Baucher's] or that it is used in excess by his adherents? As a matter of fact, Faverot never uses the word the "verticality" of the neck. He only speaks of "maximum elevation" or "the highest possible" which should be understood as a conditioned elevation; that is, the one made possible due to the conformation and level of a horse's suppling.

L'Hotte states accurately that "every horse has his notch and not everyone has a horse whose neck covers him" [a military expression to indicate the imposing height and size of the horse's neck.]

As I already mentioned, I was caught between the two tendencies, both of which seem excessive to me. The one of "B." revealed to me Baucher and his saints and made it possible for me to sufficiently grasp the [second] *Méthode*, enabling me to reproach him for making too many compromises, namely, the one by General de Champvallier and Colonel Bouhet who, with military vigor interpret the principles whose value, in reality, lies only in their nuance and subtlety.

I explain to myself their difficulties for all these reasons without questioning the talent of these two men.

This is why I am anxious to discover yet another *Baucherist*, even if he is one at only 98%, and especially when he has your talent.

2.   **Note:** PREPARING THE PASSAGE

THE MAîTRE IS MOUNTED ON AN ENGLISH THOROUGHBRED CALLED MINUTEMAN

Nuno departs with a well-sustained *rassemblé* walk, goes into a few strides of the *trot rassemblé* which, with an alternate contact of each hand and an alternate flexion of each knee, is transformed into a *doux* [soft] passage.

To animate the horse each time the impulsion begins to weaken, the rider touches behind his leg with the whip and plays between the curb and snaffle reins. It is remarkable that although the reins are never taut, there is never any break with the contact and the horse's own tension.

He now gets on the Lusitano *Allègre*. He seeks *la mise en main* [bringing the horse in hand] at the walk and the trot. He keeps a fixed hand on the snaffle, but his fingers are gently mobile. He places the spurs against the horse's hair, obtains a relaxation of the mouth and back at the walk, then at a small trot [*petit trot*], and finally at transitions between small trot, trot, and working trot. The cadence becomes obvious.

At the walk on voltes, he executes haunches-in, goes into half-passes on diagonals, and extends the trot. He returns to the small trot which he considers the reduced trot for young horses who are not yet *rassemblés*. He ends with a canter.

Now we observe a lesson on executing pirouettes. Nuno starts out performing voltes at a light shoulder-in, then haunches-in at the walk. He makes it clear that he is acting through diagonal effects, that is to say, tight voltes to the right: inside rein towards the withers and left leg slightly bent. This is the preparation for the pirouette, advancing slightly. He thus goes into a half-pirouette almost in place. He then does the same work at the trot on half-voltes, haunches-in. He ends with half pirouettes in canter, facing the corner where the quarter line of the arena begins.

Nuno Oliveira and Zurito, shoulder-in, trot *rassemblé* with great impulsion, 1965

3. Letter: SUPPLING IN THE FORWARD MOVEMENT

Nuno never condemning openly certain Baucherist principles out of fear of shocking me and my first teacher and also because he continues to have respect for Baucher and his dogmatism that verges on the religious. Nevertheless, one can read between the lines an analogous suppling in the forward movement which actually contradicts all the supplings and flexions in place taught by Baucher.

One day he makes this dazzling remark: "The benefit achieved from suppling in place is lost when executing ample and majestic gaits."

"My dear friend,

I am very pleased with the progress your horses have made during the bending lessons with regard to their impulsion and lightness. Let me assure you that there is no such thing as Academic Equitation if horses are not given a maximum of impulsion at their regular and cadenced gaits and moving in lightness. This is, furthermore, the result of the flexibility of the spinal column and the muscles attached to it.

I have invented nothing at all. I practice French Equitation, a rational equitation. It is thanks to La Guérinière, and also Baucher to whom we owe these good principles.

One must study what is beneficial in a method and add to it the best of others. I find that La Guérinière and Baucher have already discovered everything.

One must never forget "hand without legs, and legs without hand," but the flexions of Baucher do not lead to real lightness. They are a precious means to school a horse without pulling on the reins. True lightness is achieved through all the exercises and movements executed with a maximum of impulsion and the flexibility of the spinal column.

The methods are valid according to the results they obtain with a large number of different horses. I have told you that I have neither invented nor discovered anything, but the means I utilize work, for they give me good results with countless horses.

You rode *Yankee* schooled by me eight years ago, which I never rode again since then. This is proof that an equilibrium always remains good if it has been completely suppled at the outset. "Horses will always feel the effects of their initial habits." L'Hotte.

The back is very important for it is the link between the hind legs and the forelegs. Forgive me for speaking about myself and my ideas. You say that your mare has difficulties when executing the volte to the right, at the canter. Let us consider what you should do.

Depart at a very straight trot and when the cadence is good, go into a medium trot, go on to circles that are perfectly bent to the right and depart again at a straight trot with a good rhythm. Then change rein and do circles to the left, the horse well bent on the curve of the circle without letting her turn or lean to the right or the left or invert or reverse the bend.

Only when this work has been perfected will you take up the canter.

A very straight canter, then circle to the right. If she leans on her left shoulder, if she loses her regularity to the right, return to the trot to the right and the left on figures of eight until she finds her cadence again, then go back to a straight trot.

Then take up the canter to the right again, but gently without force!

I am sure that if the circle is perfect at the trot, she will also do well at the canter. This is very important.

Notify me of your results after having tried this out; I am impatient to hear about them. One should know if the horse leans on the left shoulder, going on the circle to the right, and if she does not do the same thing when going to the left?

On the circle at the canter to the left, if she does not close the volte and falls on the left shoulder, put her in a shoulder-in to the left.

The rain is preventing me from working outside and taking photos. I hope pleasant weather will soon be here. The Thoroughbred *Almaraz* is at lead changes at two tempi, very calm, and *Zafer* has begun a marvelous piaffe. *Alvito* is at the *doux* passage.

I may come to Paris in March with two horses and I hope to bring Dom Diogo de Bragança with me."

4.   **Note:** WORK ON THE LUNGE LINE

The *maître* regulates work at the lunge by means of a game with the lunge whip that is extraordinarily skillful. He uses it not only to keep the horse going forward, but also to stop him by reversing its position (putting the lunge whip in front of the horse.) Then he passes the whip again behind the horse, thereby provoking the effect of a *rassembler*, places it forward again, makes the horse step back, then [places the whip] behind and the horse piaffes.

A LESSON WITH MEXICANO,
A SUPERB GREY HISPANO-ARABIAN STALLION

At a walk, in a snaffle, shoulder-in, around the *manège* which is only 25 meters x 12 meters, riding the four corners in shoulder-in, then half-passes on the diagonal and [performs] the same exercises on the other rein.

Tracking right, he places the croup to the wall [haunches out, renvers] with left bend. At the end of the long side, the horse is straightened by the rider, executes a half-pirouette to the right with right bending, and comes back to the track where he takes up croup to wall [haunches out, renvers] again, but this time in the right bend. The same on the other rein.

In trot, at the end of the long side, a half-volte, haunches-in, return to the same side, croup to the wall, then a volte, haunches-in with a limited extension: 5 to 6 strides.

Counter-changes of hand on two tracks.

At the canter - volte, followed by a diagonal holding the haunches, counter-canter and extended canter on the diagonals.

Croup to the wall followed by half-pirouettes. Lead change on diagonals.

A trot *rassemblé* - a buck, the master lowers his hands and gives little jabs with the spur.

Andaluz, Lusitano, bending of the neck

5. Letter: ELEVATION OF THE NECK

"Work with *Andaluz* improves lesson after lesson. Unfortunately I cannot work him outside because of the rain. His walk is very good and his extensions are similar to those of *Ulysses*. He pushes remarkably well from behind with his hindquarters and bends nicely. His cadence is so good at the trot that when you come to visit us we will give him his first lesson at the *doux* passage.

I placed a curb bit in his mouth for the first time. At the canter, as with all young horses, I like to give them their freedom so that they can find their own equilibrium with gentleness and cadence.

He is so active behind that he raises the forehand with the *ramener* in a fixed position. With gymnastic exercises his withers are beginning to develop.

I am sending you some photos. Look at *Zafer* whom you know and who has a very good back. But I asked him for elevation of the neck which, I am now certain, was premature, it gave him a hollow back!

This has always been my opinion from the time we studied the photos and the books of Beudant that are in the *manège* gallery.

On the other hand, look at the photos of *Valioso* at the passage which I sent you. He has an elevation which my hand never asked him [a rejection of *Baucherism*.] This is the result of the engagement of his haunches and yet his back is not as good as that of *Zafer*.

One must have horses which are elevated in front, light, but this must be obtained through engagement of the hindquarters. and The horse must find his own equilibrium. One must know how to be gentle when helping him find it.

True lightness does not only reveal itself in the jaw. It is obtained, above all, through a suppled back which carries the weight of the rider without effort and contraction.

It is true that horses, whose necks have been raised prematurely, are not heavy on the hand, but they have an imperfect equilibrium which makes impulsion difficult as they have a locked back. Cadence of the gaits is only possible when the back is supple.

I am sending you other photos of *Zafer* for you to study. I hate them. After having looked at them, I am all the more convinced against the direct elevation of the forehand through the hands."

Nuno Oliveira, Saturno piaffe

6. Note: I CALL ATTENTION TO SOME INTERESTING EXERCISES

Along the diagonals of the *manège*, Nuno Oliveira executes the shoulder-in at all three gaits. He leaves one track at M and rejoins the other at K, at the shoulder-in on the diagonal, straightens the horse along the short side and departs again in the same manner from F to H.

He does the half-pass at the canter on the diagonal and reverses the bend as he arrives on the opposite track. He returns to the walk and departs immediately on the other lead and starts again on the other diagonal. Without interrupting the canted, on the diagonal, he goes from the half-pass to the shoulder-in, an exercise which will allow him to get the horse used to changing the bend through this lateral movement.

On little voltes he puts the horse into haunches-in at the walk, stops, departs again in walk, then to the canter.

He also executes little voltes at the shoulder-in at the walk, which he tightens into a spiral, pivoting on the horse's inside shoulder.

He begins with a pirouette at the walk and departs with a pirouette at the canter, doing a quarter of a pirouette.

It is his position which regulates the movement: bringing back the inside shoulder, outside leg is placed three centimeters back, inside leg is on the girth, total yielding of the hand.

He executes a volte tangential to the track, very bent, a halt at the *rassembler* upon arrival on the track, straight rein back.

Half-passes yielding to the leg, rein-back upon arrival on the track, on diagonals, depart at the canter, halt, rein-back, diagonalizing [the walk] while advancing.

Study of piaffe from walk, return to the trot, *rassembler* and yield with the hand, piaffe from the trot.

7. Letter: PREPARATION FOR LEAD CHANGES

"Many thanks for your letter of 9 April. Concerning the preparation for lead changes, it is indispensable that the horse be perfectly able to find his equilibrium and impulsion at the canter on the correct lead and at counter-canter, as well as on tight voltes.

Ask for transitions to counter-canter, correct canter, then in corners, also on voltes of eight meters. Bend your horse towards the inside of the volte, even at the counter-canter, but ask for the counter-canter only after the horse is well cadenced when doing the true canter.

Go through the corners at counter-canter, even bent to the inside (counter-bend.) Above all, ask for the counter-canter with active legs very close to the horse, then relax them while cadencing the canter with the seat and playing with the fingers.

If you have difficulties in your small *manège*, try this outside in a large area and begin the counter-canter in the following manner.

Begin with a correct canter and, after having bent the horse to the opposite side of the canter, execute a gentle circle on the side of the bend, and then loosen the reins.

"Ask often, be satisfied with little, caress a great deal." After having easily obtained all this in a large space, return to the *manège* and try again the counter-canter with the counter-bend. Then caress the horse and leave the reins on the neck when he goes well past the first corner.

Here is what I can say on paper (followed by a little sketch showing a horse on the right rein, bent to the left, and conversely)."

8.   Letter: DEVELOPING THE PASSAGE

Berbère was a small Lusitano horse extremely sensitive and somewhat touchy. He was probably eight years old and the master had been working him for about a year. He was beginning the *doux* passage.

Zéphir was a chestnut Luso-Arabian, very sensitive and well-schooled, whom Nuno considered more or less as my schoolmaster to study the classic airs. The idea of being given a horse already well-schooled did not bother me, since I had, upon each of my visits, the privilege of riding his personal horses. Moreover, since certain qualities in his conformation did not please me, he became the property of an American pupil.

"*Berbère* has no fear and works very diligently. I'm very enthusiastic about this horse, he is improving considerably. His passage will be more brilliant than his father's, but he lacks his regularity.

As I mentioned, *Zéphir* is progressing greatly when it comes to elevation in the passage. A few small jabs behind the girth made him move higher. I must send Abel (the master's chief groom during 15 years) to Geneva with four horses. I will also go there and then spend two days at your place upon my return. When I come back, I will send you Abel so that he can bring back *Thalar* around 20th of January."

Thalar was a superb English Thoroughbred stallion whom the *maître* had admired during a visit to the Jardy Stud farm, the famous racehorse stable of Marcel Boussac. Thanks to my friendship with the director, I was able to acquire it some time later under excellent terms and offer it to Nuno who dreamed of it.

Nuno Oliveira now answers a question pertaining to an English Thoroughbred mare, *Sensorina*, she, too, a Boussac product. I had discovered her 18 months before and he had already ridden her at my place. She was quite difficult.

Nuno Oliveira on Thalar, twenty-first ride, walk shoulder-in

"Your mare's passage: Give alternate aids with the tip of your spurs. Touch with your left spur to raise the right diagonal and conversely. Interrupt often, placing the reins freely on the neck when you feel the cadence, then start again. Insist a great deal during the whole session. Abandon all other work for a number of lessons and devote yourself exclusively to the passage. When you feel well-cadenced strides, get off her, caress her, and give her some carrots. Smoke a cigarette (!) to its end to give her time to rest. Then start again.

Before the lessons, relax her in liberty and do nothing else for a number of lessons.

Fix the hand during work with the legs, reward at the slightest sign of cadence and arm yourself with a great deal of patience.

I am sure that you will succeed after four or five similar sessions.

Note that at first you will always have a side that is easier and even a spot in the *manège* where she will cadence herself better. Prepare the suspension of the trot prior to arriving at those spots. Observe the psychology of your mare, apply yourself to her intelligence, and I assure you that you will succeed quickly. I do not know if the sessions will last long, one must expect it, but it is certain that when she gives three or four strides of passage, the problem will be resolved and you will return to the usual lessons.

Follow this [advice] and then write to me. I am sure that you will announce to me the passage of *Sensorina*. "M." will help you by observing her style and following her progress!"

9. **Note:** WORK IN HAND

May 1961

The master works a young horse in hand, on the left rein. In his left hand he holds the left snaffle rein 10 cm from the snaffle ring and slightly lowers the horse's neck. He controls the shoulders with the outside rein: the right one which passes in front of the withers bringing about the shoulder-in.

The crop taps the cadence rhythm on the flank, simultaneously keeps the haunches on the track.

The overall position of the horse is an accentuated bend, more pronounced at the neck. When I ask the reason for this flexion, the *maître* answers that at first the flexion of the neck must be more pronounced, even if it means reducing it later.

When the shoulder-in is successful at the walk, the master asks for it at the trot, keeping the same position. His main concern is an obliquity of 35 to 40 degrees, a harmonious bend and a well-marked cadence.

Then the horse is mounted, at a very free walk, long reins, the neck extended so that the shoulders have maximum freedom. He bends when going through the corners, held in check by the inside leg on the girth. Nuno Oliveira insists that riding the corner is geometrically the same as doing a quarter of a six meter volte.

The horse must not turn by means of the inside rein but by rotation of the rider's pelvis and shoulder who, in turn, maintains the contact on the outside rein.

The only role of the inside rein is to indicate the flexion of the neck to the inside, nothing more.

At the trot, at first, prepare the transitions to a more extended trot by riding in rising trot.

10. Letter: TWO TYPES OF RIDERS

July 1961

"I believe that there are two categories of *écuyers*, those who, while skilled, use the horse as a tool, and those who love him and allow him to express the brilliance of which he is capable.

The former are not less expert than the latter. During dressage tests they may even triumph although never taking the risk of making a mistake when the opportunity to yield with the hand occurs and lightness presents itself. The latter always risk being the damned poets of this art. They are misunderstood by the masses of riders who cannot distinguish between the means used by the former or those of the latter.

Only the latter enjoy the true pleasure of feeling how a creature cooperates without constraint, as a friend."

11.   Note: WORKING WITH VARIOUS HORSES

May 1963

WORKING WITH A BIG HANOVERIAN HORSE

Nuno Oliveira holds the long reins quite high and seeks a slow trot alternating with transitions, extended, then elevated. He introduces voltes, circles, and diagonals into the work.

He seeks a cadence with hands somewhat raised and has the reins at half-tension. He obtains a certain elevation and a good *ramener*, as well as a regular and elastic rhythm.

"With horses belonging to this category, who tend to fall easily into trots that are ample but mediocre, one must work frequently at transitions in a small trot, as opposed to Andalusian

Nuno Oliveira, Ansioso, Alter Real, extended trot

horses whose trots are elevated and short, and who must be given frequent transitions in extended trot to develop their amplitude."

The expression "*petit trot*" [small trot] was used by the master working with young horses for whom the term "trot *rassemblé*" was premature.

He then departs at the canter, reins long and somewhat high, alternating between several voltes and straight lines, in a free and calm equilibrium.

WORKING WITH ALMARAZ - AN ENGLISH THOROUGHBRED

The horse is light and slender. He has progressed greatly and has a regular cadence. He executes his first lead changes on the diagonal. The main impressions is that he has difficulty carrying his rider who asks him no preliminary high air. His *ramener* is becoming more pronounced, but with a slight break at the second vertebrae. I consulted Nuno about this who answers me.

"For the moment I don't aim for perfect elevation due to the weakness of the haunches and my weight."

WORKING WITH AN ANGLO-ARABIAN ORIGINATING FROM POMPADOUR
[The French National Stud that breeds Anglo-Arabians]

Work in hand, executing the shoulder-in diagonally across the whole *manège*. Should the horse resist, Nuno lowers his neck and does not hesitate bending it vigorously while keeping it totally relaxed.

"For the moment, I am not yet seeking to bend him around himself, but simply to put him in a lateral position. When he has understood the movement, I will see to it that it is done with better equilibrium."

12. Letter: THE PASSING OF A BAUCHERIST

The main character, subject of this letter, is no more. He was a horseman who was unconditionally, even blindly, devoted to Baucher, Faverot, and Beudant whom he had known and whose principles he interpreted literally. He was aware of their drawbacks, but persevered.

This letter also clarifies the conception the *maître* has with respect to exclusive [opinionated purist] Baucherism.

"I received your letter a few moments ago after having lunch with "B.", Diogo de Bragança and Guilherme Borba at the airport. I beg you to say to "B." that he has learned a great deal, so that he abandons his looped reins, the ideas of J. Pagget - (critic with *Horse and Hound*) - questions on the depart [transition] with the inside or outside leg, and all those useless questions.

I have just told him that I am satisfied each day by trying to

Nuno Oliveira, passage

find a more delicate equitation, a lightness which is a generalized suppleness, and my promptness in communicating my intentions to the horse.

If he works and follows these principles he will achieve the same results as you. He is progressing, but he must forget all the theories when in the saddle. He is pleasant, but I had to be somewhat brutal with him by telling him what I thought of his equitation and also of his practices.

I am telling you, dear Michel, that on these occasions, I feel sorry for him and I am angry at myself. If he exerts himself and works following the simple and rational methods, he will get somewhere. If he continues to dream of Faverot (General Faverot de Kerbrech and General L'Hotte were Baucher's favorite pupils), he will achieve nothing. This visit must have done him some good, in Paris he should follow your advice, for you work and ride better than him. Nonetheless, I feel sorry for him for he must earn a living and I don't think he is strong enough without our moral support. Sometimes I was annoyed by his theories and I was very harsh with him, who was my guest. He was sad and told me that he was clumsy, even during our discussions.

He will be successful with his horses only if he abandons his habits and theories. He was very concerned about the horse *Thalar*, because he felt that I did not sufficiently raise his neck and that I did not have the reins looped. He has undoubtedly seen this very complicated stallion ridden in the arena, reins in half-tension, amongst the other stallions that were evolving around him in all directions!

He is also concerned with what I write in my book saying that "the hocks must meet the mouth thereby adjusting the reins for you!" He thinks that this might create bad results with the readers! I answered that I was not writing in imitation of Faverot, nor publishing photos in the style of Beudant.

What I am doing, what I claim to do, delivers results. This discussion will remain between us and this letter is only for you. Let us forget these complications and try to cadence the passage of *Andaluz* by slowing him down, especially with direction changes, so that we can begin working him at the piaffe when I will be at your place."

13. Note

July 1962:   WORKING WITH *VALIOSO*,
PUREBRED ARABIAN OF BAD CONFORMATION

Nuno executes numerous transitions between extended and small trot, not to speak of the *rassemblé* trot, for which the horse is not yet ready. The half-halts used in order to encourage upward-stepping in the trot is punctuated by halts destined to improve the *rassembler*.

He then goes into shoulder-in at the canter, on circles, searching for an extension of the neck, forwards and downwards, by engaging the seat and lengthening the reins. He looks for cadence at the gaits towards the *rassembler*, his hands are quiet and immobile, but his fingers strum the reins alternating with gentle legs.

In conclusion,
Impulsion + Slowing down on beat = Cadence.

14.   Letter: BIOGRAPHY

I seem to remember that the biography the master is referring to and asked me to edit. It was destined for the magazine *L'Eperon* [The Spur].

"Only today did I received your letter with the biography, which I do not deserve, but which I find very well done. I don't think anything else should be added and I am somewhat confused.

Currently I am working very hard with seven of Borba's colts, plus four more in the stable, the rest are my horses, and we have many foreign visitors.

People from the Philippines bought M. Resina's grey horse. I still have the time to ride *Thalar*. He is doing well. He is almost at the canter in place and his two tempi flying changes are exceptional. When it comes to the piaffe and passage, he is progressing, but I push him very little in these airs, for he knows them and it is useless to tire him doing them, especially in this hot weather.

Joao looks forward to going to Bailly. I will send him to you on 3 August. Let us talk equitation. With Minuteman, English

Dr. Guilherme Borba, at home. Student of Nuno Oliveira, director of the Portuguese School of Equestrian Art

Thoroughbred, I work more the left shoulder-in that the right, and each time he throws his head up and to the right, I stop him right away and make him do a left shoulder-in. I return to the right shoulder-in and start again.

As to what you consider cold [not reactive] to the legs concerning *Andaluz*, rest assured, when I will be there [at Henriquet's place.] We will tackle the piaffe, which will transform his sensitivity.

Your concept of academic equitation as an equitation of delicacy and gentleness is correct. You can be satisfied with it, and of all the French horsemen I know, you are one of the rare ones who have understood the nature of equestrian art."

15. Note: A SHOULDER-IN LESSON

1963

In the corner preceding the long side, the *maître* rides a six meter volte which gives the horse the desired bend for the shoulder-in. He keeps the bend along the wall at a 40 degree angle by keeping the horse on almost four tracks.

He explains, "Once the horse is placed at the shoulder-in on a straight line, the dominant aids are the outside rein, which regulates the shoulders more or less inward, according to its needs, the inside leg at the girth which keeps the haunches on the track and accentuates the movement of the inside hind leg in front of the outside hind leg.

One can say that the outside rein controls the forward third of the horse and the inside leg controls the two thirds of the horse behind. The shoulder-in is composed of an obliquity which can go from 30 to 40 degrees with respect to the wall, a harmonious bend of the entire horse, a cadence which, especially at the walk and trot, gives it all its value.

The role of the inside rein is merely to preserve the light flexion of the neck, nothing more. The role of the outside leg is merely to maintain the haunches with a slight bend.

The master then states that with this horse which is difficult to bend, he will use the circle for the shoulder-in. He places himself on the circle, first on one track at the trot. Progressively, he lowers his inside hand, after having opened it a little, which positions the horse. With his inside leg at the girth, with the aid of the whip, he pushes the haunches a little outside of the circle described by the forelegs.

He determines the circle drawn by the shoulders with the outside rein slightly open, and controls the bent haunches with his outside leg slightly back.

Continuing in this position, he goes into canter and continues the exercise of the shoulder-in on the large circle.

Andaluz, Lusitano training the piaffe

16. Letter: TWO FRENCH RIDERS

In this letter the master calls to mind two French riders who visited him on my behalf. Commandant Bernard de Fombelle, an extraordinary show-jumper, a person of distinction who, as soon as he had learned the principles of our school, never ceased to apply them to his jumpers, and Commandant Jean Saint Fort Paillard, *écuyer*.

"Sunday, I went to the Santarem Fair where I did not see a single horse worthy of looking at. I told you that I would go to M. Ervideira, breeder of *Beau Geste*, who, I understand, has four three-year-olds who are very handsome.

The son of breeder Palha wants to sell me a young horse at a reasonable price, so that I can have a horse of his at my place. I looked at his horses returning from Santarem but I was not carried away. The day after tomorrow I will have lunch with his brother, a very pleasant and original man who wants me to give him a lesson in the shoulder-in!

I very much like the work your *Zéphir* does. He already executes a few pirouettes and his piaffe is very promising.

Zurito, the horse I bought from Manuel Veiga is transforming himself and begins to walk with his back. Trying to de-contract him is very interesting.

Ulysses is in great form and *Fombelle,* fascinated, has just worked with him. He is a very intelligent chap and a remarkable horseman. He understood what was exceptional about *Ulysses* and his schooling. Unfortunately the horse has a problem with his right hoof and when it becomes painful he contracts and places his poll the wrong way. His work then becomes imperfect. When he is well, I believe there is no horse capable of working as well, as lightly, as relaxed, with such feline-like movements. He walks using his back and all his tension pushes him forward from behind.

Fombelle took maximum advantage of him and has ridden him like nobody else. Observing this intelligent horseman with *Ulysses* every day this week gave me tremendous pleasure. He has immobile hands and his back remains in perfect accord with the horse's back as he works him. He was able to take advantage of all this.

On the other hand, Saint Fort Paillard, who is not at all steady on horseback, neither with his hands nor legs, bothered the horse *Ulysses* would not accept the movements of this rider who inconvenienced him. That is all.

Meanwhile, I have received a long and friendly letter from him on equitation wherein he claims that he is in accord with me! Well, my dear Michel, what we need is to ride and have results. It is easier to succeed with words than on horses.

Monsieur Thalar, whose piaffe is now twice as good as it was on the picture that I sent you, is making tremendous progress. I now ride him in the arena even while clients and pupils are moving about without him losing his equilibrium.

How are your horses? I count the days till September when I shall have the pleasure of being with you and help you to improve, also with the schooling of *Andaluz*. We will accomplish another phase. I have already thought about what you will do when I get there.

Have you seen Fombelle? He wanted to see you on his way back to talk and to observe you on your horses. I told him that you were a French disciple.

I am trying to find you a decent young horse and will send you the papers so that you can fill out the import formalities."

Nuno Oliveira with *Ulysses* in passage September 1962

17. Note

1963: STUDY OF PASSAGE AND PIAFFE
WITH A FIVE YEAR OLD

Starting with a trot as slow as possible without losing cadence, Nuno Oliveira supports his outside rein, pushes his seat forward, and engaging his lumbar vertebrae, he lets his "soft" leg (this is his expression) touch the horse's sides. What was a little trot, similar to a school trot, becomes a *doux* passage. The strides of the horse are lightly suspended.

He remarks that at this stage he does not seek the elevation of the strides, but simply a decent diagonalization wherein the hind legs do not remain behind.

To prepare for the piaffe, he starts off again with the shortest possible walk, taking care that the horse does not remain in place. When he goes forward again he tries to execute strides that are still short and regular.

When he obtains one or two movements in place, he goes forward, sometimes at the small trot, while keeping the horse on the bit, as rounded as possible. He does not hesitate to let the neck lower itself in order to retain a high [withers] dorsal arch. He holds the upper part of his body somewhat back, the pelvis engaged. He alternately places his spurs against the horse's hair, making sure his legs do not touch the flanks. It is a true caress with the spurs. Three or four times on each rein, separated by extended walks and lengthening of the neck, on long reins.

A lunging lesson -- The tip of the lunge whip is placed toward the extremity of the tail when all goes well. Directed at the girth when the horse tightens the circle and Nuno Oliveira wants to widen it, under the arm if the young horse rushes at the canter. Use of the voice with a brief tone for upward transitions and a low tone for downward transitions.

He moves the horse to the corners to reduce the diameter of the circles, describing voltes of 6 to 8 meters, then returns to the center to widen the voltes into circles of 10 to 12 meters.

After executing one or several circles at the trot as cadenced as possible, he asks for extension along the track, letting the horse straighten himself.

To do this, he yields with the lunge and accompanies the horse who lengthens his strides. He returns to the circle, and then once again asks for extensions at the trot on the track along the wall.

Impostor in passage, 1972

18.   Letter: ADVICE ON THE PASSAGE

During an international equestrian event it Lisbon, Nuno Oliveira entertained several jumping riders who came to see his work at his home. The group included Fernando Sommer d'Andrade, one of Nuno's first supporters, a great and important breeder, a man of culture and a competent observer of the equestrian discipline. Between the master and Fernando ,a solid friendship developed, which does not prevent frequent taunts occurring from both sides.

"I am delighted that you are pleased with the presentation of your horse *Andaluz*. It is thanks to your work with him. Continue, and you will arrive at some very good schooling.

These past days I received some riders in international jumping. Captain D. greatly appreciated my method and told me that he would like to have an outstanding show jumper schooled by myself! He rode several of my horses. Fernando d'Andrade came with them to give them a lesson. One of them asked me if he could ride *Thalar* which I could not refuse. They found him tremendous. But I assure you that I was so upset that I could not eat.

I believe that there are very few people who are sufficiently sensitive to ride well-schooled and sensitive horses and that they do not even try to understand and feel them. They are incapable of following and staying on the back of a horse.

D. told me that I ought to teach French Equitation. French or Chinese equitation just the same, *haute école* equitation will be practiced only by half a dozen chaps throughout the world.

One can win at important dressage and jumping events, even become a champion, but to ride with the light brushing of the leg, the buttocks well placed in the saddle and steady, the hand fixed and light, is seldom seen.

I gave a lesson in the shoulder-in to D. who thought he knew how to do it. He understood it at the end of the lesson. Tomorrow we will see what he has understood. As a show jumper he is tremendous. He jumped beautifully with *Zaire*, but as a dressage rider he is a zero. However he is an open-minded chap who wants to learn.

Fernando found him to be very good, but I assure you, my dear Michel, I suffered.

This will be the last time that anyone rides *Thalar* or any of my personal horses, at least those who have not worked with me for some time.

I now feel like riding quietly alone. Excuse me for bringing up all this nonsense! All the riders are convinced that they are the best. Only he who wishes to practice this art in all its purity and who loves and understands his horse knows that the latter never flatters him and immediately indicates his slightest faults.

Plutarch was right when he said that "Equitation is what teaches a young prince best because his horse never flatters him."

What is interesting about equitation are the results which the trainer perceives and not that which attracts the crowd.

Dear Michel, how many times do I get off a horse feeling a great sadness and feeling very unhappy? It is because of this mixture of suffering and happiness that equitation is such a passionate art. Excuse me for opening myself to you like this.

I shall write to you again this week to let you know what kind of young horse I can find and send you. As far as the passage executed by your mare *Sensorina* is concerned, here is some advice to enable you to go from the insufficient cadence you have, to the trot *rassemblé* and to the passage. Teach her the *jambette* as you know it, along the side of the wall, on each rein. Then ask for the *jambette* along the side of the wall, from the trot; trot, halt, and immediate *jambette*. Change rein. When she gives it to you in a good cadence, reward by letting go of the reins, start again, and you will have the passage. Since she already somewhat knows the *doux* passage, with the *jambette* she will raise the diagonal higher with cadence. Ask often, be content with little, caress a great deal!

Au revoir, I shall ride *Thalar* for my pleasure."

Nuno Oliveira on Thalar, Thoroughbred stallion, half-pass

19. **Note**: REMARKS BY THE MASTER

1964

"With the shoulder-in the horse can leave the track with the shoulders, the haunches, or both. If it is with the shoulders, without pulling, tighten the fingers on the outside rein, if it is with the haunches, keep the inside leg more forcefully on the girth. Never pull on the inside rein, which only indicates the bend of the neck, and hold the haunches with the outside leg 3cm [1 inch] behind the girth."

Nuno Oliveira goes through the corners at shoulder-in which is a more elaborate exercise. Riding corners forces the horse to slow down his shoulders while the haunches describe a quarter of a pirouette.

I notice that the *maître* holds his whip, most often on the right side, placed above the right knee and directed towards the sides of the horse. He uses it by making a rotation of the wrist.

20.   Letter: MISUNDERSTANDINGS

Here is a long letter written in one of those moments of enthusiasm and fury provoked by the lack of understanding on the part of certain people. The immense talent of Nuno Oliveira, the extent of his equestrian culture, his experience, raises him to a level equal to no other.

The problems that he faced, the solutions that he brought to them, often went beyond the boundaries of well-known treatises, but were always justified by common sense and his results. When he had to deal with questions asked by a few learned men about such and such an author, even classical, about the method he used or the position he worked the horse in, and noticed a criticism or even a remark, he held his irritation in check, but worked off his anger on those close to him.

The following letter is such an example. "B." is this Baucherist of whom I have already spoken and with whom I had worked for several years before discovering Oliveira. "B." never hid his admiration for Nuno, yet never ceased to deplore everything that was not in the direct line of Baucherism. Furthermore, Nuno suspects him of having complained to me about his work with certain horses. This is too much for him and it is an explosion wherein he holds "Beudant, etc. etc." up to public disgrace. It is amusing to stress that in his fury he does not dare mention the name of Baucher himself. Yet it is he who is designated by the terms etc.

Rightly or wrongly he never worked with horses of great quality for financial reasons as well as looking for difficulties which he considered a challenge to surmount. While he was able to criticize himself and his own horses, he could not accept criticism when it came from horsemen outside of his school and his philosophy. One must investigate the reason for his irritation when someone calls attention to his horses' weaknesses.

"After having spoken to my son Joao during dinner, I am convinced that "B." wants to persuade you that *Ulysses* goes from bad to worse. I had a discussion with this poor fool "B." with respect to *Ulysses*. He was of the opinion that the horse was doing worse because I work him with a lower neck. Fernando d'Andrade, who was present, agreed. He cannot stand it when I work horses from stud farms other than his. You know that I am neither thickheaded nor an idiot and I know better than anyone else the defects of *Ulysses,* whose poll is sometimes turned when executing half-passes to the right, has poor style at the canter, a regular, but slow, piaffe... not a single person can remedy these defects. On the other hand, his immobility, his *ramener,* his cadenced and vibrant gaits, all belong to a horse working with his back. His true lightness, his school walk and trot, his Spanish walk, the lightly jumped rhythm of his passage, his half-passes at the passage, are all rare. His serpentines at the rein back, execution of the Spanish walk backwards and the regularity in all his work, few horses are capable of giving these things.

This is also the opinion of Borba, Diogo and the professor. I have undoubtedly schooled other horses to a higher level, but I am not ashamed of *Ulysses* and am waiting for these critics to present a horse like him.

"B." should first learn how to ride in a relaxed position, which will help him arrive at the *rassembler* before communicating his opinions to us.

I know what defects this horse has. Nevertheless, I know what his good qualities are. It is easy to criticize when one does not know how to surmount difficulties.

The schooling of *Ulysses* separates me more and more from Faverot, Beudant, etc. etc. and comes close to the ideal I have in mind.

My good Michel, do not let yourself be influenced by a miserable chap who knows about equitation only what he learned from books.

He finds *Thalar* on his shoulders, but I do not want to elevate his neck at this point. He has only had six months of schooling. *Zéphir* disappoints him. I would like to see if he could have cantered him with the calm that he now shows in his mouth. If his passage is not very elevated, it is because not all horses achieve this. *Zurito,* whom he likes a great deal, raises the diagonals quite high due to contraction but without engagement. Frankly, yes, he came to teach me and not to learn. Let me tell you that he rode badly, that his fall from *Lidador* is that of a rider who lets his horse, without any impulsion, do little jumps in place. Let him read Fillis and his quote from the fable of *The Fox and the Raisins* [ref. Aesop's fables, sour grapes.]

Ulysses is not an event horse. He is an artist, who, despite his weaknesses, works with a rare equilibrium.

Please forgive this little angry "anti-B.", but I have less and less patience with this type of person."

In this letter one can clearly see the purpose of the master's quest and how far he has moved away from the preoccupations of contemporary dressage and its criteria. His horses of the time, despite certain functional and locomotive inferiority, surpass some of those who were further schooled, but less brilliant and light. He will never cease to search for this ideal equilibrium.

Rath Patrick was a Canadian horse, a champion an the Pan-American Games with Patricia Galvin, a pupil of Nuno Oliveira at the time.

Finally, the *maître* wants to de-mystify the belief which says that all well-known *écuyers* are capable of training all horses to the same level.

"I intend on presenting *Ulysses* and *Beau Geste* in Paris. I will be at the disposal of connoisseurs in your *manège* to demonstrate what I am looking for. I know what I want, just as I know how to criticize what I do not like in my work.

I continue working along this path, searching for an always superior equilibrium and lightness.

In the past, I schooled horses who executed airs and gaits which *Ulysses* and *Beau Geste* cannot obtain. The lead changes of *Almondo* and the mare, *Silène* were superior to those present at the Olympic Games in Rome, as Guilherme, who was there, can vouch for.

Well, I believe that the equilibrium of *Ulysses* and *Beau Geste* is greatly superior to that of these horses. *Rath Patrick*, despite his impeccable tests, is incapable of executing a good passage and a good piaffe. This is due to the horse himself. If one wishes to teach everything to each and every horse, one ends up with a grotesque pantomime, with certain airs that have nothing to do with the beauty of the Art. My Master Joachim Miranda said that "In equitation everyone feels that he has the right to consider himself competent, but only real *écuyers* can really judge."

I put you in the class of those with whom I like to talk, whom I like to hear and teach. I know horses' defects. I correct them when I can, as far as nature permits me to do so, but then I must content myself with the maximum a horse can give me. One must not spend a lifetime trying to change a horse's nature, hoping to find the ideal, which is very rare. Each horse has his qualities and defects. The history of perfect horses is only found in books!

For example, *Thalar*, who does outstanding work at the trot and canter and has a good piaffe, will never achieve the kind of passage that *Ulysses* can. On the other hand, I am sure that *Mick* will have a very good passage but a considerably inferior canter to *Thalar*.

Why did Beudant not give to *Hamia* the same piaffe he gave *Vallerine*?

Do you think that Jean Saint Fort Paillard is clumsy to the point of not being able of improving the piaffe of old *Patrick*? No, the horse cannot give a better one.

With *Ulysses* I could remain with a piaffe-like movement, but what purpose would that serve if he cannot piaffe high and slow? Baucher says that not all horses are able to give a piaffe that is high and slow.

Why does Beudant publish only two photos showing those airs with the arms raised almost horizontal?

Why does his horse *Vieux Jeux* not have a brilliant and elevated movement?

Will you be able to give *Sensorina* the same elevation at the passage that you give *Andaluz*?

No, that will not be your fault, for it is physically impossible to achieve it with your mare. Why do you prefer her half-passes? Do you think that it is because "B.", as a pure Baucherist, had you first do the half-passes without first going through the shoulder-in? No, it is because the rigidity of the spinal column of this Thoroughbred mare facilitates the tension of the back, in contrast with the excessive mobility of the spinal column of *Andaluz*!

In short, one must give each horse all the brilliance and perfection that his whole ensemble entails."

Nuno Oliveira on Saturno, Lusitano/Arab in piaffe 1958. "The lowering of the haunches provides the support to enable the raising of the forehand."-Nuno Oliveira

21. Note

A YOUNG HORSE WHO IS STILL VERY APPREHENSIVE GETS EXCITED AND RUSHES CONSIDERABLY AT THE CANTER

Nuno Oliveira first lunged the horse for a fairly long time at the canter on circles (more than six meters), alternating with voltes (less than six meters) in order to calm him. He mounts and says that once mounted, he will abstain from doing voltes at the canter, but will go around the *manège* to prevent the young horse from putting too much effort on his hocks at the canter.

I note that on this horse Nuno holds his hands very low and quite forward on the reins. The elbows are placed close to the body. The application of "hand without legs and legs without hand" is evident; I would even say "fingers without back; back without fingers." He pushes his upper body upwards and lets his legs lie gently on each side of the girth. The [rider's] lower back, the lumbar part of the spine, is slightly arched and the seat is quite open and relaxed. His head is always tipped slightly forwards as though to compensate for the relaxed engagement of the loins.

22.   Letter: CRITICS

The *maître* had presented *Euclides* at the *Gala de la Piste* at the *Cirque d'Hiver*. He had not ridden him for over a year, having sold him to a charming friend but a very whimsical horseman. I myself was quite worried when I found out that he could only practice riding him the evening before the presentation. In a word, I was opposed to this dangerous performance due to the risk to his reputation. It was filled with difficulties due to the state of confusion into which the horse had been put by the new owner in an attempt to teach him the levade!

Like so many other letters, this one reveals the state of anguish which often took hold of Nuno Oliveira. His precarious financial situation combined with mistakes he sometimes made with respect to his behavior, often put him in situations from which he could not always get out without getting hurt. My admiration and affection for him prompted me to warn, and even reproach him. He accepted this badly, and justified himself by giving specious [appearing to be true but really false] arguments, such as "who could perform better under such circumstances or with this type of horse?" Our disagreements reverberated around these explanations which his pupils and especially his public could not comprehend.

Aware of his enormous talent and undoubtedly also of the many mistakes which spread confusion among his admirers, he reacted defensively as seen in the following letter.

Francois Cuyer [trainer of various Olympic riders] was an old *écuyer* who, at the time, was the only one in France who could make horses piaffe and passage. He had succeeded in making the horse *Cramick* execute these airs. *Cramick* had been French Dressage Champion with Colonel Braux.

"Why did I not piaffe at the *Cirque d'Hiver* with *Euclides* who was able to piaffe previously and is able to piaffe now? Because I did not want to risk appearing grotesque with all this levade business. I could present him now, as in my former presentations, at the piaffe/passage transitions with the kind of perfection which had been noted in *L'Année Hippique* [a Swiss annual magazine covering all the main competitions of the year.]

True *écuyers* command attention by their very work - the

critics demolish. Connoisseurs understand and appreciate each other, even when their methods and procedures differ. For this reason "B." is shocked because I admire Cuyer who does not work the way I do, but who demonstrates results that are difficult to obtain.

As a matter of curiosity, look at the two photos of *Ulysses* at the passage which appear in my book. There is a year's difference between them. Then compare them with the photo I shall send you. In his Baucherist idiom, "B." prefers the first one which shows an extremely raised neck and this damned pigeon throat. In the second one he is already less tied-in, his ears point forward, the cannon of the foreleg advance, and he is more engaged and *rassemblé*. In the third photo, the neck is more extended; he is less constrained and really goes forward in the passage.

The poor blind chap prefers the first one! His seat is more accustomed to riding mountains of books than the back of suppled horses.

Today Guilherme Borba told me that *Ulysses* rushed the Spanish trot; I agreed with him and corrected it. It was the correct criticism of a rider who can discern a correct movement from an incorrect one.

What is wrong is horses not working in the position of the *ramené*, who lash out when they feel the spurs, who are rigid in their gaits, who are loosely held [not on the bit], in a false lightness, whose loins are hollow and weak, and who raise their neck against the action of the hand.

Constant perfection, that is the ideal, but it is not for us mortals. Beethoven wrote divine music but also some compositions that one can criticize.

You will see, my very good friend, that you will be praised by idiots such as "L.", criticized by senile equestrians such as "B." and "A.", and appreciated in your difficulties by the Borbas, the Bragancas, [*Dressage in the French Tradition,* D. Diogo de Braganca, Xenophon Press 2011] the Oliveiras and by your *écuyer* friend at the circus (Alexis Gruss, Sr.), all of those who themselves have encountered difficulties schooling many horses.

Difficulties do not lie within the methods, but the particularities found within each horse which can be either partially or totally resolved.

Many years of schooling can lead to the rin-tin-tin of routine, on dormant horses, or more or less spectacular frolics, without achieving equilibrium and lightness. What is really important are harmonious movements and perfect relaxation between horse and rider.

In Étienne Beudant's book, [*Horse Training: Outdoors and High School,* Xenophon Press 2014] do you prefer *Mabrouck's* backward trot or the ease with which he jumps in a Moroccan *douar* [village]?

I do not want to overwhelm you any more today. I hope to see you soon riding your horses, to correct or praise you, and understand your difficulties."

Euclides, Lusitano, passage. *Gala de la piste*, Paris 1966

23. Note

THE MASTER IS AT WORK SEEKING THE *RASSEMBLER* WITH AN ALREADY ADVANCED HORSE

He keeps his upper body held slightly back and his elbows somewhat away from his back. His legs are gently caressing, his relaxed ankles regulate the slight brushing of the spur.

He prepares his canter transition from walk, having first regulated the horse's equilibrium at the walk through his position. His upper body is immobile; the direction of his inside shoulder directs and supports the outside hand. He achieves cadence at the walk by supporting the outside rein, keeping the inside leg at the girth and, still with an active and cadenced walk, the outside leg moving forward, as though "stroking [the hair] the wrong way," he strikes off into canter.

He gives the canter's tempo by engaging the sacrum in a more or less pronounced manner, going forward from behind, joined by the cadenced enveloping movement of the upper legs. His outside hand gathers and regulates the motion of the canter. The reins remain at the neck, his inside leg, immobile at the girth, forestalls any deviation of the haunches.

To execute voltes, he does not utilize the inside hand, and turns, almost without the effect of the reins, with his shoulders and his pelvis. His hands are almost joined, using only his fingers to take and yield.

His outside leg holds the haunches slightly bent, the fingers of the outside rein limit the fold of the neck. His shoulders are completely quiet.

At the counter-canter he retains exactly the same cadence he had in true canter and allows no rushing. He slightly turns his upper body towards the outside. He then executes a half-pirouette towards the corner of the *manège*, turning shoulders and pelvis towards the angle and caressing with his outside leg held somewhat back.

To execute rein changes he bends the neck after leaving the corner or after doing a half-volte, pushing laterally with the seat and outside leg, slightly holding the horse's shoulders with the outside rein.

Nuno Oliveira, Euclides, Lusitano, pirouette

24.   Letter: PRESENTATIONS IN ENGLAND

In London the *maître* presented his horse, *Curioso*, an excellent Alter Real whose schooling period had exceeded three years, and which had caused some to remark about this. Always sensitive to what could appear as criticism, yet all the while affirming his detachment, he cannot avoid a minor defense *pro domo* [for one's own benefit] which I extract from one of his letters.

"In all my presentations with *Curioso*, The English public applauded me with enthusiasm and I will be able to obtain the film from the BBC.

Do you think that with more years of schooling I could have executed better pirouettes, even with respect to lead changes, extensions, and the two tracks? He was absolutely calm, regular, and light.

I understand less and less how people can talk about equitation without showing anything. They talk too much.

Years and years of prolonged schooling by the so-called *maîtres* is often due to their incompetence and conveniently removing this good creature's impulsion to the detriment of its sensitivity.

What I find sad is the attitude expressed by French equitation for which I'm fighting and which is represented by Germanized judges who understand nothing about equitation.

I received "B.'s" letter asking me to continue in the idiom of Baucher and Beudant and to abandon the shoulder-in. How crazy people are!"

25. Letter

"The English press made a great show about my performances. I could not have done any better with an older and more schooled horse, with the exception of *Curioso's* piaffe which is not outstanding but superior to many of those seen at the Olympics. Monsieur Smith Jenssen asked me to return to England. My aim is to present an artistic equitation which is exactly what former French equitation had been and I regret very much that it has been forgotten in your country and replaced by the new German equitation. I also regret that the French equestrian press publishes idiotic articles which do a disservice to French equitation."

Zephir 1963 schooling the passage

26. Note: ADDRESSING LEANING ON THE SHOULDERS

The *maître* rides a client's horse which has not yet attained the *rassemblé*. The horse leans on his shoulders and weighs heavily on the rider's hand. Nuno begins by putting the horse forward at the walk without using his hand, and then progressively takes him up again without using his leg. As soon as the horse begins to hold back, the leg intervenes once again, the hand becomes neutral, but held low.

The aim is to obtain the yielding of the poll and lower jaw, that is to say, to prepare him for the *mise en main* [bringing the horse in hand.] The same work occurs at an energetic trot, first rising, then sitting trot, but hands always low. Then halts from walk and trot, on the snaffle, searching again for the *mise en main*, that is to say, the yielding of the poll and jaw without inverting the roundness of the neck. The master proceeds in place, using what he calls little jabs which are more akin to vibrations with the leg, almost becoming slight brushings with the spur. As soon as the horse yields, he moves forward in a *descente de main* [yielding with his fingers on the rein.] He is applying one of the most interesting of the Baucherist exercises for tense horses.

Then, at the trot, he raises his outside hand on reins which he calls "soft." The neck is more supported, as is the cadence of the trot. As soon as it is lost, he returns to the preceding transitions.

He executes voltes in a right shoulder-in which he terminates with some strides at the half-pass with the same bend. Confronted with an increased difficulty, the horse rushes forward somewhat, but he soon puts him into haunches-in on a volte, along the long side, so that he can become calm and cadenced again.

These exercises continue also at the canter around the *manège* which he terminates on a large circle, covered at least ten times. Progressively, he lengthens the reins up to the seams, the neck lowering itself, forward and downward. The seat replaces the hand; the horse's back is raised and relaxes completely. He terminates by going large at an ample trot, first rising, then seated, and finds himself in a new cadence and lightness. He says to me "It is after a session at the canter like this that one can achieve the best kind of trot."

27. Letter: THE RIDER'S SEAT

"Your letter reached me on the eve of my departure for Australia. I am thus writing to you from the end of the world. I was very satisfied with your work and that of your pupil, Catherine.

With respect to the rider's seat and the parts in contact with the horse, when working the *rassembler*, all depends on how he flexes at the level of the sacrum.

He must have his buttocks engaged under him and well set; he must engage his lumbar vertebrae forward and downward so that the lower part of the pubis is in contact with the saddle.

I am sending you the measurement of my legs for the gaiters. Madame H., who is coming in September, can bring them to me."

28. Letter: FLYING CHANGES

I am having difficulties with flying changes on a Thoroughbred and I am asking the master for help without realizing that my approach by letter concerning a horse he has never seen, is somewhat childish. Without riding him he cannot evaluate my mistakes and inadequacies. Nevertheless, he answers, working out my most likely errors and he is quite correct.

"Are the shoulders and haunches of your horse, Minuteman, perfectly straight as he departs at the canter to the right and to the left? From the walk and from the trot?
Is his contact with the snaffle equal and soft on both sides? Is his contact with the curb bit on the right side harder and does it bend the middle of his neck to the left when you ask him for the departure to the right canter?
Does he give you a well channelled impulsion and at the same time the possibility of vigorous transitions from the working canter to a canter that is somewhat *rassemblé*?
If any of these problems arise, correct them first before going into lead changes.
I will now give you the means of approaching them after you have settled the rest:
You depart at the canter doing a volte to the right, coming out of a corner of the *manège*, before getting to the short side. Halt your horse in the middle of the short side, rein back three or four steps, ride another transition to canter on the short side. Make another volte, slow down the canter and halt on the volte, in the center of the next long wall. Rein back three or four steps and take another departure.
Do this ten times, twenty times, or one hundred times if necessary, until the horse does it in perfect obedience, with a gentle contact and an impeccable *rassembler*. You will feel how he cadences more and more with impulsion.
When all this has been perfected, you ask for flying changes first in a corner, then in the center. Act with the left rein placed against the neck and receive the horse's neck on the right rein. If there is sufficient impulsion, the lead changes will be easy. Courgeon,

who came here with his horse, is making sensational progress. In ten days he obtained lead changes at three tempi and has begun the passage and piaffe.

I am overwhelmed with work, my horses are progressing, and your friend Bienaimé is sensational!"

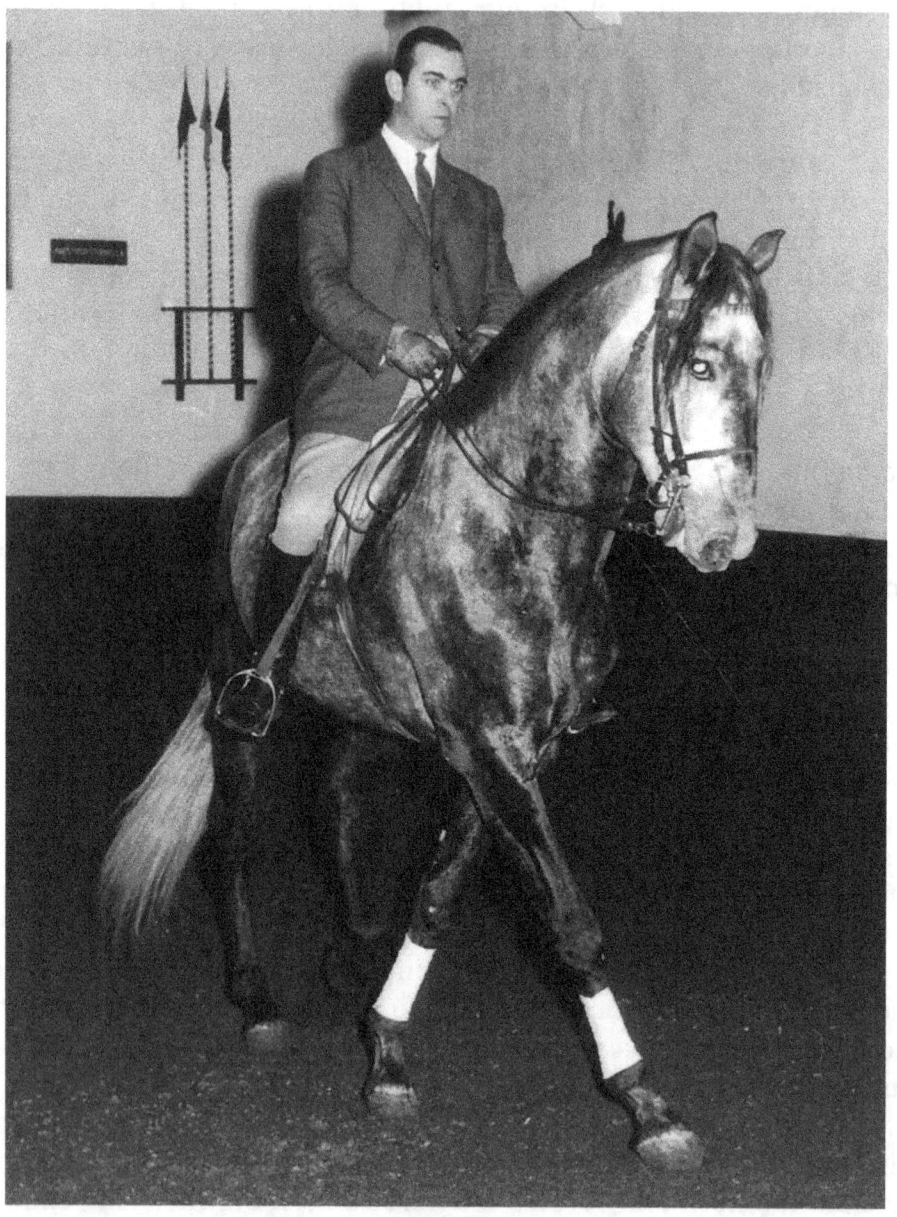

Half-pass

29. Note: PREPARING A FIVE YEAR OLD HORSE NOT YET *RASSEMBLÉ*

This pupil's horse leans heavily on his shoulders, is heavy on the hand, and is in a constant state of imbalance.

The master halts him as regularly as possible, making him place his fore and hind legs together in increased engagement. With the aid of light touches from the spurs, he carries him forward, supporting the snaffle rein and the neck, the poll is relaxed; he then yields with the fingers, the horse moving forward *en descente de main;* that is, with fingers relaxed on the reins in lightness.

As soon as he begins again to be heavy on the hand, Nuno tries to balance him again by holding his hand higher on reins that are gentle but alert. Then, from a halt he goes backwards two or three steps in lightness, and then forward again.

He begins a volte of five or six meters at the shoulder-in, which he pursues. He then reverses the shoulders towards the outside of the volte, holding the haunches towards the inside.

The horse rushing, despite being subjected to variations in his equilibrium, he continues unperturbed at haunches-in, with head and shoulders parallel, along the long side, thus re-establishing a reasonable cadence.

Commentary of the *maître*:

"With this kind of problem, one must avoid as much as possible using one's hands, and instead use the action of the seat, be it for changes in direction or preparing exercises, or for example using the legs alone when executing a half-pass, a caress with the opposite leg holding the haunches.

The whip or a long whip gives precise but gentle touches, may be quite effective if the leg is not heeded."

Nuno Oliveira on *Zurito* in a canter pirouette

30.   Letter: IMPULSION

"I hope that in a week I shall be able to tell you when I will be in Paris.

To work your horses well, never forget that they must always be in a state of permanent impulsion and must never be behind the bit during exercises. Otherwise, they will be in a false lightness. Impulsion is regulated by a hand that does not feel any resistance.

You must hold the reins at a semi-tension only with certain exercises that are very *rassemblés* and when you want to school your horse giving him superior impulsion. Everything else is a false lightness. Thereafter, examine the engravings of the elders, look at their reins, their bits, look at the kind of impulsion they have and then ponder over it.

True impulsion is the possibility of taking contact with the bit, a gentle contact, with a *descente de jambes* [yielding of the legs.] *Zurito* works that way almost all the time. He is at the piaffe and is beginning lead changes.

Our friend Guilherme Borba has been drafted as veterinarian, and will be in Africa two months from now. I received two very poor photographs from General N. which included very kind words. Poor equitation!

Do not be concerned about my health. I am in good shape, full of energy and impulsion."

31. Letter

THE MASTER ANNOUNCES THE PURCHASE OF A YOUNG HORSE OF WHOM HE GIVES QUITE AN ORIGINAL DESCRIPTION.
IT MUST HAVE BEEN *EUCLIDE,* WHICH WAS ONE OF HIS BEST-SCHOOLED HORSES

"I am answering your letter somewhat belatedly. Riding and the problems that beset the many horses that I am working do not leave me much time, and when nine o'clock in the evening arrives I am so tired that I dine and go to sleep.

Zéphir is progressing. From time to time, I already feel the same *rassembler* at the canter to the right, (the more difficult side) as in the canter to the left. Professor J. da Costa, who rode *Audaz* at the same time, found that he had good lead changes. I am not yet satisfied but know that in time, with tact and patience, I will succeed. *Audaz* deserves it, as he is so very handsome. What interests me above all is to resolve the problem of the *rassembler* to the right, for his right hind leg begins at times to have the same gentle action as he has to the left. The right shoulder-in at the canter helps me considerably.

Monsieur Thalar is starting to be valiant in his haunches and courteous in the mouth" [an 18th century reflection that a horse should be dynamic in his hindquarters and light in the mouth.] His work at the walk is ample and his cadence is remarkable. He is well positioned at the *rameneé*, ears pointed, reins held semi-taut.

I have already obtained the canter departures, I tried the counter-canter, which went well. He still grinds his teeth, but considerably less. Impulsion will eliminate this vice.

Yesterday there was so much impulsion in his trot and it was so supple that he fell into a few strides of *doux* passage. At home Joao says wittily that he is my fourth child.

In England I saw many lovely Thoroughbreds, but *Thalar* is superior to them.

The day before yesterday a Danish *écuyere* came here. I asked Abel to start the music. I rode *Thalar* and entered the *manège* at a school walk, executed counter-changes of hand on two tracks, halts and departs from the walk to the *trot rassemblé*, extended and shortened trots and canters, reins on the neck. Voltes at the canter and counter-canter. He worked impeccably.

Fernando Andrade, who was present, told me that, despite his desire to tease me, he could not find a single fault in the work.

I have just bought a young horse from him which has a very nice color, good movement, an atrocious head and the body of a giraffe. We shall see how he will develop. I sold two part-breds who will travel to Switzerland with *Berbère*. Thérésa's chestnut and the one of Madame Gandrup are beginning to do lead changes at tempo. Branca and I are delighted to see you at our place. It is a condition *sine qua non!* [without which, there is nothing].

Ulysses, Spanish trot

32. Note

HERE THE *MAITRE* RIDES A NEW HORSE THAT TOSSES ITS HEAD AND FORCES THE HAND

With each resistance, Nuno gives the horse a fleeting touch with the spurs, starting with a gentle pinch [progressing] to little *attaques*. He determines his actions on the strength of the horse's defences. He then stabilizes his hand on the snaffle rein and anticipates, if necessary, the use of the curb rein. He maintains the horse at his gait, and does not tolerate any modification.

He frames him within a channel of aids, which, he claims, is a channel of silk. That is to say, it is simultaneously a gentle and channeling force, adhering, more than ever, to "hand without legs, legs without hand" and "forwards, always forwards."

This horse has already acquired quite a technique of resisting and the treatment he gets from Nuno Oliveira is more coercive than the kind he would have given to a young horse who would resist due to poor balance and inexperience. Here the defenses are marked with a certain malice.

The master then asks me to ride a five year old horse that begins to go from a trot that is somewhat *rassemblé* to a *doux* passage. Under his direction, the lesson I give this horse prepares him for the passage.

I go from a working trot to a *rassemblé* trot, almost raising his limbs, coming close to a *trot rassemblé*. I develop impulsion over three or four strides and with a half-halt on the left rein, given just when the left diagonal is raised, I try simultaneously to slow down the stride and to give it a moment of suspension. Alas, I provoke more *precipitation* [loss of suspension, rushing] than suspension. Nuno says to me "the horse's legs transmit messages to the hands of the rider through his back and his seat. Thus, engage your loins more, make your legs soft and relaxed, and let him come to you until the spur first strokes the one side of the horse then the other without force. Do all this as you yield on the rein. A horse can neither passage nor piaffe when he is on the bit [with a strong contact] without falling into an ataxic [losing muscle coordination] cadence."

33. Letter

In this letter Nuno Oliveira refers to J. Pagget, editor of *Horse and Hound* [British Equestrian Journal], a faithful supporter of our ideas who had written a controversial article for *L'Eperon* on the decadence of modern competitive dressage in answer to articles by Messieurs Aublet and Challan Belval, the auguries [technical authorities] at the time.

"Can you send me the article by Pagget in *L'Eperon*? I find it good and wonder how Aublet and Challan Belval will answer it.

I have also prepared an article for *L'Eperon* which I can illustrate with some photos.

Let us now speak of your horse *Andaluz*. Head to the wall [haunches-in or travers] at the canter. One must not abuse this exercise. It is excellent for suppling the haunches but, if abused can make the horse crooked when one wants to canter straight on the track. One must limit the use of this exercise and alternate it with shoulder-in at the canter. As a consequence, the quality of straightening will give you the exact measure to be used.

To execute it, put yourself on a volte at the canter, well bent on the short side. Profit from the bend which the volte requires to begin with head to wall on the long side, holding with the inside leg. Once arrived at the end of the long side, straighten, and on the short side, on a well curved circle, execute a semi-shoulder-in. When doing the head to the wall exercise, give a few touches with the spur on the inside [inside leg to the lead] so that he can engage more fully the inside hind leg. This is also a good way to prepare for the pirouette.

Is your mare *Sensorina* any better? Mastrangelo is a great veterinarian, I am sure he will cure her.

I will continue this letter this evening, after the lesson on *Thalar* whom I ride after teaching the "college children" at two o'clock.

[Later] I just had some passage strides resulting from *Thalar's* good and well-cadenced trot and impulsion.

I assure you, my dear Michel, that I can show you as high a passage on a Thoroughbred, who brushes close to the ground, as one can on an Andalusian. I am not exaggerating. I am satisfied remaining with a fixed hand and supple fingers, relaxed, well seated, taking advantage of his equilibrium. One must allow the horse to act on his own.

Thank you, thank you with all my heart for this wonderful *Thalar*. I am ill and my illness is called *Thalaritis!*

In London I rode a Lipizzaner who had been schooled by the Vienna School, then given to the Mills Circus. Madame Hall, the international champion had ridden it without any good results, not even a canter transition. I analyzed the horse, mounted, and executed the whole repertoire. Quite astonished, the English ask me how I had done this. I answered: "One must use neither more leg nor more hand than is necessary."

It is the same with *Thalar*. My hand never opposes his formidable natural impulsion, my legs do not annoy him, and he is happy in his work.

These principles should be applied to all horses: minimal aids, no forced raising of the neck with the hands, shoulder-in, voltes, many voltes, hands always immobile. Baucher and Beudant are in agreement about the immobility of the hand. What they have written about elevation was only to fill the pages of their books and trouble the Champvalliers, the Bacharachs, etc. etc.

The fixed hand is all that is needed. The main thing is that it must be stabilized in relation to the rider's supple loins. If the rider has loins that go against the horse's back, the hand will always be in opposition. Think about this...

The horse's supple back, the supple lower back of the rider, the fixed hand, thus supple, that is everything in equitation.

I, myself, am aware that when I am tired and my back aches, my hand is poor. On those days, I shorten my stirrup leathers and do the rising trot, reins long, to give the horse his exercise.

All this, added to the principle: **ask often, be content with little, and caress a great deal,** produces a well-schooled horse. Of course, there are difficult horses. But even with them one must apply the same principles. It takes longer to school them, but when this method is applied, at the end of their schooling one obtains really suppled horses.

Artificial means are good to wow the ignorant and fool ourselves."

Nuno Oliveira on Violaceo in passage in the presentation for the riders of the Spanish Riding School July 31, 1963

34. Note: COPING WITH WEIGHT RESISTANCE IN THE HAND

The master has to cope with weight resistances, that is to say, when the horse lets his head and neck be carried by his rider's arms or has strength resistances. When the horse's mouth clearly pulls to avoid the hand or to carry it away, he applies little jabs with the spur, keeping a fixed hand.

As the slightest yield, he relaxes his fingers. This is the famous "take and give."

Here he is executing the passage on a circle and recommends turning without using the hand which breaks the cadence. Turn with shoulders and pelvis, the horse does the rest.

He recommends doing more half-passes, haunches-in, as they are described by La Guérinière and at the wall at the end of the track, a half-pirouette, returning croup to the wall [renvers]; at the trot and canter at the end of the long side, execute a half-volte, haunches-in, and return parallel to the long side, croup to the wall. These exercises complement the shoulder-in. The lengthening of gaits must be prepared by their cadenced elevation, especially at the trot and canter. This tends to make the horse's *ressorts* [resilience and pliability of his muscles and joints] tense and increases their efficacy when relaxed.

To extend the gait, he makes a sign which the horse recognizes. Nuno Oliveira advocates either a quick and precise touch of the whip behind the leg or a slap with the two calves which continue to adhere to the sides of the horse in order to assure the fixity of the seat during extension. As long as the horse is not *rassemblé*, he allows the neck to extend slightly in the extended gait.

35. Letter: BAUCHER AND THE SCHOOL OF VERSAILLES

The letter below clearly demonstrates the extraordinary understanding Nuno Oliveira has between the two methods which are the basis for Equitation in the French Tradition. The authors and best-known practitioners of these two schools have never been able to bring about a clear choice which could have resulted in a corpus of important and coherent doctrines that the upper echelons of present-day equitation still lack. The works of La Guérinière and Baucher have been constantly placed in opposition to each other without anyone ever taking the trouble of holding them up to each other and comparing them to see to what extent they complement each other.

It is true that Baucher cut himself and his own equitation from any ties with the Equitation of Versailles. None of our interpreters saw to what extent the Baucherist contribution, once free of the allurements that the master had slipped into his work to impose the postulate of his exclusive originality, could be included into the immense richness of the *Grande Ecurie* formulated by La Guérinière.

Those who worked with Nuno Oliveira for some ten years or more, those who saw, read, and heard him, will agree with me that the title of "Restorer of French Equestrian Art" should be given to him.

"I do not agree with Beudant in one respect, namely when he says that the *ramener* is not indispensable to the schooling of the horse. The horse does not possess a perfect equilibrium unless he is *ramené*.

What is necessary is not to seek the *ramener* by direct and static means, but through gymnastic exercises in the forward movement, through the shoulder-in and suppling the back, for it is then that the horse will inevitably fall into the *ramener*.

My dear Michel, the valuable and rare pages that La Guérinière wrote on equitation are more timely than the thousands of pages written later by people such as Raabe, Fillis, Saint-Phalle, Salins, and all the others.

Baucher is not so far removed from the spirit of La Guérinière. If he wanted at all cost to write about a method completely different, what he actually sought to achieve was the lightness of La Guérinière.

It is within these two great masters that one must find information that is profitable to art. "It is lightness that gives to *Haute École* equitation its true cachet and true character of his talent to the rider who practices it." [L'Hotte]

"Only when one works in lightness is one truly involved with equestrian art. The rest is the massacre of the innocents.

Do not stray from these principles. Continue working in lightness and you will achieve the stamp of French Equitation.

A horse acts proudly when he is happy doing the airs. And when he is happy, he will not be tense and will move with suppleness.

It is useless to discuss the simple contact with the reins at a semi-tension with those who do not understand the meaning of equitation. It is futile.

A horse who has supple reins, back and hocks is *rassemblé*. The reins can be adjusted with a contact that is merely the result of their weight. The croup must push in such a way so that the mouth of the horse takes contact with the reins.

It matters little whether the reins are more or less loose the moment when the horse maintains contact without being heavy. There must be no leaning on the bit.. The horse is balanced when there is no weight resistance or force. His back is supple and the *rassembler* eliminates all contractions.

Any problem with either mobile jaws or inert ones is a false problem, and depends upon the temperament of the horse. Only the absence of resistances counts."

Nuno Oliveira, half-pass 1963

36. Note

A NEW WAY OF ASKING FOR YIELDING OF THE JAW

Working in hand, on the left, holding the curb rein in the left hand, raised, and the snaffle reins in the right hand, lowered. Whip in hand, an aide gives little taps on the croup until the horse yields his jaw and poll.

The actions are combined but opposed, moving downwards with the snaffle and upwards with the curb, yet combined in the mobilization which is almost in place and provoked by the whip; they are a sort of *effet d'ensemble* which loosens contractions [rigidity.] Then, continuing in hand, holding the two curb reins in the left hand ten cm from the bit, with marked lightness, the rider, facing the left shoulder, puts the horse into a smaller, slow and cadenced trot. He provokes and maintains impulsion with the whip on the horse's sides until he obtains a *doux* passage which he shortens to obtain three or four strides that are very *rassemblé* and then moves forward.

**Nuno Oliveira on *Euclides*, Lusitano in passage,
"Fête du Manège"**

37. Letter

I received this letter upon the *maître's* return to Lisbon from my place where I had presented him to about two hundred figures who represented the equestrian world in 1969.

During this meeting, Nuno Oliveira had shown films and, after being asked, still in his city clothes, he rode one of my horses, which provoked a strong and admiring reaction, at a time when no competitive European horseman could show a balanced horse or when the FEI was considering suppressing the piaffe and passage from its main competition tests. M. Renom of France, president of the Federation, telephoned me a few days later to thank me, saying "I want you to know the comments made by General Noiret, *Commandant* of the *École de Guerre* to the *Commandant* of the *École de Cavalerie de Saumur*, with respect to the presentation of your *maître*. At a dinner which I attended, I saw this week a young brilliant Portuguese horseman to whom you should send your *écuyers* so that they can learn how to ride."

This wish was practically granted years later when General Durand, then Colonel and *écuyer en chef*, [at the *École de Cavalerie de Saumur*] had the bright idea of calling upon Nuno each year at the *École*. To those who never knew him, this letter might appear as an expression of total pretentiousness, but to us it expresses one of those moments of exaltation which seems ironic.

In the eyes of the insignificant admiring disciple that I was, he wanted to confirm his discussion and, if necessary, assure me that I was not mistaken!

Those who consequently saw *Euclide* and his other horses can testify that the touching pomposity of this document in no way exaggerated the extraordinary schooling of his horses.

"I am writing to you this morning at six a.m. between working two horses. I ask you the following questions:
1) Do you believe that tempi lead changes in the corners and on the small sides [of the *manège*] are as easily obtained by the horses of "B.", "S.", and "G.", as those you obtained with *Euclide* and *Chaimitte*?

2) Do you think that at *L'Étrier* ['The Stirrup', France's most prestigious equestrian club] there are horses as capable of doing, as they are, two or three figures of eight with one tempi lead changes, without missing a change with a hind leg?

3) Do you think that after a pirouette, slow or fast, these horses can immediately take up changes at tempo as *Euclide* can?

4) Do you think that with *Euclide* I could be able to imitate Fillis and do tempo changes along several hundred meters on a race-track?

    Do not bother with critics of that kind. I proved that your schooling was not bad when I presented your horse in front of this Areopagus [reference to the Athenian supreme tribunal] of horsemen and it is after having ridden him that the Austrian *écuyer* wrote his good article and that General Noiret, a practicing horseman, made those positive reflections.

    After presenting the films, I critiqued myself in front of your invited guests. The position of my legs surprises them. You know that I do not want legs that are clamped on. Their relaxed state allows me to have a *rassembler* that is somewhat superior to the ones obtained by these poor guys!

    When I work my horses during presentations, I want no one to see either a leg or a hand move. Ask Bienaimé who, when he was here, said to me that he could not understand my aids, for my horses worked without them!

    I purposely prepared this little theatre to astonish him.

    As for the pirouettes at the canter, according to the classics and even the Federation, the horse must maintain the rhythm of his *rassemblé* canter. Explain to me why almost all pirouettes executed by these people are done with neck and head movements, and, moreover, lose their cadence?

    If you had studied this kind of equitation, do you think that you would be at the level at which you are now and which gives me such pleasure? You have been working seriously at academic equitation for a relatively short time. You should be pleased with your results.

La Guérinière considered Andalusian horses as the finest and most subtle, as did all those subtle *écuyers* living in more refined times. The artistic feeling of these horsemen I have seen in France is weak, for, using artificial means, they prepare inappropriate products from the race track: the English Thoroughbred with his natural rigidity.

That type of horse is better suited to their type of constrained equitation than are the mobile and *rassemblé* Andalusian horses. How poor art is under such conditions.

Have no fear. I will continue practicing the equitation which, I believe, comes closest to that of the elders. The other kind does not interest me and even bores me.

I am writing this letter to you in the best of spirits and with great calm, with a heart filled with friendship for you and right now regret the 2000 km that separate us.

Zurito is expecting me at the *manège*. I shall ride this generous horse, reins in my left hand and whip in the air, with lightness and well *rassemblé*."

Nuno Oliveira on Zurito in the canter in place to the right

38. Note: TRAINING FLYING [LEAD] CHANGES

First, one must put the horse in a true relaxed state and with abundant impulsion. Nuno stresses that subtle aids will have no impact on a rigid horse that canters without spirit.

"To prepare the lead change from right to left, one must accentuate the action of the left leg prior to executing the lead change until the last moment. If the horse is just being introduced to lead changes, it is good to get him used to cantering first with a slight counter-bend only at the neck, the body very straight, and to give him this slight counter-bend on the left lead, a few strides ahead of the lead change. This will prevent him from being worried about the change of the bend imposed upon him just at the moment of the lead change, which is often the cause when executing a lead change at two tempi.

A horse well impulsed by the left leg, neck lightly bent to the left, one uses the following aids: right buttock and leg, holding on to the right rein so that when changing it does not deviate to the left.

At first ask a great many lead changes, but always in an easy cadence. Press the rein on the base of the neck on the side of the lead asked."

The *maître* then works at a slow canter to prepare for the pirouette which necessitates, at the start, a canter that is almost in place.

He asks for half-passes on the diagonal at the *rassemblé* canter. Arriving in this fashion on the opposite track of the *manège* at the counter-canter, he goes on to a slow canter holding the horse straight. He supports the forehand with the outside rein of the bend, closes his fingers on light reins in the ascending phase of the canter stride and then yields in the descending phase.

With the same cadence, his legs envelop the bulging part of the flanks. At the slowing down of the canter, haunches are low and the forehand sustained, which is obtained and regulated more by the rather deep engagement of the seat than by the actions of hand and leg which disturb a precarious equilibrium.

39. Letter: LEAD CHANGES FROM RIGHT TO LEFT

I had written to Nuno about my difficulties with respect to lead changes from right to left with a young horse. I remember now that I had neglected the preparation of the light bend of the neck before going into the lead change and it is with respect to this correction that his advice was worthwhile.

The horse *Damasco* became very restless when my leg came in contact with him and to avoid worrying him I rode him with my seat, legs somewhat distant. Looking back, I realize the error and impasse when one acts in this manner which never solves the problem. The horse must accept the leg as communication, and it is this lesson with the placing of the leg that the master writes about.

"I received your letter yesterday. Here are my answers to your two questions:

B) Left Lead change
One cannot say that the lead change from right to left is the most difficult one. This depends upon the horse. The same horse has a phase when a lead change on one side is more difficult than on the other. This may change and return when on the other rein until the horse is straight, well *rassemblé*, and goes forward.

In your case: Activate your left rein placed against the base of the neck and somewhat from left to right and very lightly from front to back. Activate the rein for just a brief moment before beginning your leg action.

A remedy for the same situation: often ask for lead changes to the left while you are working on the right track to go into counter-canter. Once you have attempted these two remedies and the horse has improved his lead changes, use your aids exactly the same way on both sides; that is, keep a good contact on the rein of the lead asked. Do not let it go.

C) *Damasco* is easily irritated by leg action.

It is a case somewhat similar to that of another horse, *Corsario*, but easier. One must get him used to caresses with the spur. He must accept when you move your legs along his flanks and approach your spurs to his coat. You must apply these progressively without frightening him. Rather, this should calm him.

You must arrive at the *effet d'ensemble* of Baucher, but always keeping your spurs well forward. Then you will have him depart from walk to trot, well cadenced and *rassemblé* by increasing the contact of your spurs. You will attempt this procedure from the girth to the flanks.

The main thing is that the transitions occur with a good *mise en main* [bringing the horse in hand.] Only then will he become calm. Stabilize your hand, fingers gentle, put him well forward and back on the bit. Yield when the horse is already moving and above all, keep your legs relaxed, yet enveloping, seeking the most possible points of contact between your legs and the horse.

This work must also be done at the half-pass. When he has become calm, do some transitions at extended gaits, all the while yielding the hand, the horse free.

Here, my dear Michel is what I advise you to do in this case."

40.   Note: EXERCISE FOR A FOUR-YEAR-OLD HORSE

As soon as he is in the saddle, Nuno Oliveira moves the horse at an ample and free walk, neck horizontal and relaxed, maintaining cadence and amplitude through the engagement of his seat. He goes into a relaxed trot, after having slightly adjusted the snaffle rein to preserve the contact with the horse's mouth, the neck having risen slightly. He allows the neck to remain relatively free, yet maintains the horse stretched by means of a strong impulsion.

From halts, he asks for lightness by playing with his fingers and tension in his back, alternating with circles, voltes and slight extensions on straight lines. He insists on the geometrical regularity of the figures which "inherently school the horse."

He executes lateral movements by bringing the young horse on to the center-line from the middle of the small side, and putting him into a semi-shoulder-in towards the far end of the long side. I call these "demi-diagonals at the shoulder-in."

To move past corners he pushes the horse with his two legs, indicates the bend with the inside rein, compensates by supporting the outside rein and tells me that his inside leg is like a column around which the horse passes, between the corner and this "column." For him, the corner is one quarter of a six meter volte. He executes figures of eight and gentle shoulder-ins on the long sides.

The aids for the shoulder-in are mainly the outside rein which regulates more or less the positioning of the shoulder-in and the master's inside leg at the girth which holds the haunches.

The inside rein is secondary and merely indicates the bend of the neck as is the outside leg which bends the haunches.

"Never allow the horse to rush. Should you feel that he is glued to the wall, hold him with the outside leg and bring the hand towards the inside."

"On circles, if the horse takes a false bend, lower the inside hand and jab delicately with the inside heel while holding the outside lateral aids [hand and leg]."

"Regulate your weight it the turns, press on the inside stirrup if he leans into a false bend [too much bend in the neck,] touch with the inside spur and support with the outside rein."

"Do not bend sideways, but turn your shoulders with those of the horse."

"Alternate extensions with slowing down without going out of cadence."

"Should he resist when doing rein changes, touch with the spur or give a half-halt upwards."

"To return to a cadenced working trot after an extension, close the fingers with gentle hands, seek the deep part of the saddle, then cadence: legs without fingers, fingers without legs."

After giving these recommendations, the *maître* departs at the canter. Hands are discrete, thighs relaxed, the movement is indicated by the lumbar muscles to the seat, to the coccyx, and transmitted to the back of the horse.

To depart at the canter, one must wait until in the cadence of a slightly raised trot, in a corner, the inside leg at the girth and the outside leg behind it, which gives the signal to move forwards, "stroking the wrong way." With young horses, The master always ends his lessons at a trot with a good rhythm and at the passage with the more advanced ones.

A five-year-old on the lunge. Nuno wants a calm warm-up, and then holds the lunge two or three meters from the cavesson, and with the lunging-whip pointed towards the haunches, gently mobilizes the croup, maintaining the shoulder-in on the circle, on each rein, at walk and trot.

When I ask about the possibility of jaw-flexions, he answers in the negative, saying that "the horse has a talkative mouth" [he is too mobile in the mouth.]

He then mounts and works him at very extended gaits and on very long reins. "The horse sways [floats in his direction], I do not hold him back, but I give him an additional amount of impulsion which tenses him and I center him in the channel of silken aids."

Nuno Oliveira, *reverence*

41. Letter: THE IDEAL OF *HAUTE ÉCOLE*

The "few notes" of which Nuno Oliveira speaks are his "Reflections on Equestrian Art" which had already been published in Portugal and which will be published in France in 1965.

"I thank you for your letter on d'Aure's book, and the two opuscules [minor works] on Baucher which I found very interesting. I asked René Bacharach to translate some notes I have written and hope to make them part of a little edition, adding to it other pages that are now ready.

Ask Bacharach to show them to you. They represent my opinion on dressage and certain problems that arise.

They are addressed to riders who like academic equitation and appreciate working with a calm, light, and brilliant horse.

I find that the ideal of *Haute École* is to have a horse that is calm, but also light and balanced, so that he can give "all the brilliance that his ensemble can encompass." E. Beudant.

True lightness does not only lie in the yielding of the jaw. It also includes absence of resistances, impulsion, equilibrium and brilliance.

Without lightness none of these conditions can be achieved. Unfortunately, the schooling that one observes today during official dressage shows no longer has anything in common with academic equitation. It is bad circus. They show horses who are 'routinized', express no grace, and for that reason the public is losing its taste and interest in *Haute École* equitation.

In this art, as in all the other arts, one must have "beauty" for without it there is no art.

Show the public, even those not well-versed in equitation, horses who are supple, light, and brilliant. The eqitation will immediately be appreciated. If you present work that is dull, mechanical, without beauty, only two or three persons will be interested, no more. Equestrian art must not be lost. It belongs to our culture and to European civilization."

42.   Note

"The position of the leg must be stabilized by the knee, resting gently on the bulging part of the flanks, by the part situated between the hock and the heel, feet parallel to the horse, without excessive tension on the stirrups. This allows him a relative stability.

One must alternate the use of the curb rein and snaffle rein. It is necessary to vary the cadence of the gaits often, from the most extended to the halt." -Nuno Oliveira

The *maître* works in hand, on the left. In his left hand he holds the snaffle reins 15 cm from the mouth, and also holds them in his right hand [at the buckle] towards the horse's shoulder.

He makes circles and voltes alternating with shoulder-ins on the track, interrupted by *rassemblé* halts on the track.

Once mounted, at the walk, he multiplies voltes and pirouettes, advancing amply [with big strides], the preceding in haunches-in. He does the same at the trot and canter, alternating between trot and canter on the track.

Preparation in hand for the Spanish walk. As was done earlier in hand, on the left at first, he holds the rein 15 cm from the mouth, then gives little taps behind the forearm while keeping the horse going forwards, even if the horse raises and bends his foreleg a little. He begins again on the other rein.

43.   Letter

"Program for your rigid Thoroughbred.

"Start shoulder-in at the walk, along the wall. At the end, turn in the corner on a volte: without changing the bend of the neck, continue on a serpentine, always at the walk. The horse must turn at each loop of the serpentine, while preserving the same bend. Guide the horse well with the seat and legs to prevent him from slipping sideways. Always at the walk, cross the *manège*, diagonally, at the shoulder-in, then relax the reins and allow the horse to de-contract [relax] at an extended walk.

Do the same program on the other rein. Then do the same work at a small trot, on each rein. End up with a counter-shoulder-in around the *manège*.

With all these exercises keep a permanent and regular cadence. When the horse has obtained a good rhythm in a vigorous trot and obeys the light touches of the reins, try to depart at the canter before reaching the corners. Then go on from the trot to canter, from canter to trot, on voltes, well bent by the lateral action of the outside aids with reins at a semi-tension.

The moment has arrived for getting the horse used to the spur near the girth at the halt in complete immobility. Gently increase contact with the spur near the girth, letting go when the horse advances quite straight and free. [Faverot de Kerbrech's *Methodical Dressage of the Riding Horse*, OBEDIENCE TO THE LEG AND THE "EFFET D'ENSEMBLE" ON THE SPUR page 11, Xenophon Press 2010.]

Now seek the *ramener* through a succession of voltes that are very curved, shoulder-ins and counter-shoulder-ins at the trot. Work these exercises as soon as possible at the trot after having worked them well at the walk. Do a great many trot sessions while seeking impulsion and the beginnings of the *rassembler*, very little at the walk.

I received a letter from Commandant de Fombelle who is delighted with his visit at your place, and the same from Commandant Padirac. They ask me equestrian questions to which I must answer. I await Patricia Galvin who will be coming with the prince of the *Tour d'Auvergne*.

My son Joao is very happy that he will visit you in August.
I told him that next week, as soon as he has finished school, he was to come each day to the *manège* to learn how to ride well and be in good condition so that he can help you with your horses.

How is your thoroughbred? Does he have a hot-blooded or a cold-blooded temperament? Give me details about your work and do not hesitate to ask me questions."

44. **Note:** *MICK* AT WORK, A FOUR-YEAR-OLD ENGLISH THOROUGHBRED BELONGING TO A CLIENT

He is four years old and has been worked for twelve months. He is elegant but seems rather stiff.

His walk is ample and energetic but the neck is stretched forward without the *maître* intervening to try to flex poll and jaw by direct actions of the hand.

He repeats voltes and in the corners he executes tight half-voltes while holding the haunches, which make the of the horse's poll yield on gentle reins.

He ends the half-voltes, haunches-in, with a few half-passes towards the wall. He does the same exercises at the trot, goes into shoulder-in on half-diagonals from the center of the small sides at A and C, towards the middle of the long sides to B and E. Starting with voltes of six meters in diameter, he executes haunches-in along the long sides with an obliquity of 35 degrees, head and neck parallel to the wall. *Mick*, despite his obvious difficulties due to the natural equilibrium of a handsome race-horse, yields with enough good grace to the virtuosity of the *maître*. It is a good exercise of style.

A few remarks. Nuno's hands are low, level with the bottom of the edges of his jacket. Above all they are absolutely immobile, elbows rigorously held at his flanks. One notices only very little isolated actions of the aids, but, rather, a unique kind of aid, body made of one piece (*in monobloc*), with not a single part separated from the rest, entirely connected to the impulsion, movement, and balance.

When I transcribed these lines, thirty-five years separated me from the date when they were first written in my notebook. Since then, I saw and studied all the masters in this discipline, be they international champions or *écuyers* from world-renowned schools, but never have I met a rider whose fusion was as complete with the horse as an extension of himself. It was impossible to discern where lay the will of the one and that of the other and determine its structure. The mythic centaur, fabulous personality, halfway between man and animal, was facing us.

45. Letter: WORDS OF A CRITIC

This letter deals with an equestrian critic who wrote under the pseudonym of Sobène Olstef who was actually a former cavalry officer who had worked with General Decarpentry. He was very kindly disposed towards us, but ferocious with the horsemen of that period and always pushed us ahead all the better to demolish them.

"Your horse is handsome and well-schooled. He is an excellent teacher, but has not yet reached that level at which you can show him to those people who consider themselves well versed in the art. Hold on to him for a while for you must refine your equestrian tact and ride with the precision close to a millimeter. Then you will sell him for a large sum because of his lovely coat and beautiful mane!

I was reading the articles by Sobène Olstef in *Plaisirs Équestres* and became aware how childish people are in their understanding of lightness. It is not because the reins are more or less adjusted that one can see if a horse is more or less light. It is because of his overall carriage, the flexibility of his back, his supple and harmonious movements.

I mentioned this in an article in *L'Eperon* "The hocks meet the mouth and regulate the reins for us ! ! [A convergence of forehand and hindquarters] They can be taut by the simple weight of the leather, or semi-taut with a fixed hand. That is all, the hand never pulls."

Neither must one, my dear Michel, fall into the opposite error of those riders who want their reins to be taut; they pull. These two defects are also bad. The reins and the legs must be gentle. On the photos I sent you, look at the extension of the trot. The reins are adjusted, the horses have a relaxed back, ears are pointed forwards, and the hind legs are engaged. The hand is fixed relative to the rider's flanks and the latter is flexible in relation to his relaxed back. Compare this photo with the one of the horse belonging to S. and his extended trot which appears in the last issue of *L'Eperon*. You will see that with my horse it is the hocks that meet the mouth and adjust my reins.

Add this photo to the others for the article in *L'Eperon*. Many thanks."

In the following letter, the *maître* evokes an *écuyer* who is very pleasant, very honest, who admires his equitation and its results, but who cannot admit that his equitation no longer contains a trace of Baucherism and its methods, such as suppling in place, elevated neck, etc. This attitude is interesting, for since the expansion of the Baucherist method in the nineteenth century, it was the method used by a number of French *écuyers*, both civilian and military, for whom the passage, through the raising of the neck and head with raised hands, and the horse in place, was inevitable to achieve the *rassembler* through lightness.

It is precisely for these excesses that the Germanic *écuyers*, contemporaries of Baucher, always adhered to the *École de Versailles*, condemned Baucher, accusing him of being the grave digger of French equitation.

"I received your letter of 15 September. Yes, you are correct. "B." is very nice, but has understood nothing. What he wants, what he likes, is not to ride and balance horses, but convert people to Baucherist theories.

He told me that last year *Ulysses* was better positioned when he had a pigeon throat. I told him that this year, with a neck that is more flexed, he was more channeled and obedient. He admitted to this, but regrets that the horse no longer has a pigeon throat!

My English Thoroughbred is naturally on his shoulders and at this stage I avoid asking him to raise his neck. Nonetheless, I am very pleased with his progress and I assure you that I do not want him to raise it much more.

I raise *Zafer's neck* and he moves poorly. In this position it will be difficult to solve his problems at the canter and lead changes.

"B." prefers finding a justification for his confused theories, and I am not interested in hearing them. What has always interested me is schooling horses following the most natural principles. He who notes the horses' daily progress but finds another method preferable, is not very intelligent. He has an inverted culture and that is all.

You discuss, you ask questions, you act, and that is why you improve your results. Dear Michel, in equitation one must be like Saint Thomas: seeing before believing.

I hope to continue teaching what my long experience and my successes with horses have given me.

Let us leave poor "B." alone, who gets on our nerves with his special aids for the canter and his pigeon throat!

Come soon for I need to talk with you. Here I have Borba who always agrees with what I say and do, but who talks little, and there is Théréza who is similar.

Among the books you have, continue studying Steinbrecht. [*Gymnasium of the Horse*, Xenophon Press 1995.] He is perhaps somewhat difficult for fluttery minds, but fortunately this is not the case with you.

Tell me if my son Joao has really done something positive with M. Volpi's horse. I am very interested to know what he has achieved.

To me, equitation is something so important that I become merciless with those who do not want to practice it in all its purity and I am always less inclined to teach them.

My old *maître,* Miranda always said that horses are much more intelligent than their riders and learn with greater docility."

46. Note: REMARKS

To do the half-pass, Nuno does not move his hands at all. He adjusts the reins in advance which enables him to obtain the correct bend without pulling on the inside rein towards the withers. His outside rein does not move, he is satisfied with closing his fingers to slow down the shoulders.

If he has a problem doing the half-pass he does a half-volte haunches-in, by turning his shoulders, and takes up the half-pass again.

He is on a horse belonging to a pupil and who, due to his gaiety and defense, lowers his head at the canter, leaning to the inside. He raises the outside rein, moves it somewhat outwardly with vibrations while keeping the head straight and bent at the corners with his inside hand. He steadies his inside leg and avoids tightening the lower outside leg.

Each time he recovers a good equilibrium, he pushes the horse forward by means of his back and seat.

For a horse that leans into the volte at the canter and loses the neck bend, he holds the whip vertically against the inside of the neck, vibrating it, so the horse can straighten and the correct bend can return. He also supports the outside rein to avoid the break in the neck, actually turning his volte at the canter with the outside rein, only his seat assuring the correct bend of the ensemble of the horse on the circumference.

Preparing a horse for a presentation, he should be lunged a few hours beforehand with side-reins, with a great deal of impulsion, and have him execute small voltes of 4 to 5 meters in diameter, more at the canter than at the trot.

When a young horse at the first stage of work leans into the volte when reaching the track, raise and move away the outside rein, using the inside leg to keep the horse along the wall; to leave the track, turn the seat making the bending the neck slightly with the inside rein. Ride with a lot of impulsion.

Nuno Oliveira on Thalar, pure thoroughbred, the *doux passage*, [soft passage] 1964

47. Letter

"When are you coming? It will do you some good to work with my horses. It will be good, for you will feel new sensations of impulsion.

How are your lead changes doing? Do not forget to hold your horse perfectly parallel to the wall and remain well seated in the saddle.

If the right hind leg arrives at the second beat at lead changes to the right, go into a lot of shoulder-is on circles and voltes in the right canter.

Stop for a while doing successive lead changes and with this preparation through the shoulder-in, be attentive to single lead changes. Do not worry. Your problem is that of every *écuyer*. One must always return to simple basic exercises, to the straightness of the horse, and to good and equal [symmetrical] single lead changes.

You can always draw upon the semi-shoulder-in [shoulder-fore] and shoulder-in to equally engage, each hind leg.

To go back in your training to correct, is to perfect the exercise that the horse already knows, but which must always be improved.

As to the polemic with Commandant Licart, I am totally in agreement with you. Nonetheless, I advise you to let these people write without getting into a debate with them.

Be a philosopher. These discussions only give fuel to the editors allowing them to fill their pages.

Men like Licart, Pagget, Sobène Olstef, all these chaps have never properly ridden a horse, never schooled one. They write to let off steam and end up fooling their naive readers. It is a fight lost in advance to want to change them and even useless, for they are themselves, not convinced of what they are writing about since they never really practiced it. Then they become furious and malicious!"

48.   Note: WORKING WITH VARIOUS HORSES

To start out a young horse at canter-transitions from the walk, after a halt on the diagonal at X, ask him for a departure on the other rein, and then take up again on the other diagonal, and so on. This assumes that he already departs with ease along the wall. It is this exercise that the master has just done with a five year-old.

He then executes half-passes at the most shortened canter possible, on short diagonals, halts and departs again, parallel. He indicates that, in a while, the next stage will be the counter-change of hand at the canter with a very brief departure from the walk, from the left to the right and from the right to the left.

With another horse, the master alternates at the walk then at trot, three to five strides at haunches-in and as many strides in croup to the wall [haunches-out].

He then works a five year-old horse in hand. Cavesson and nose band in front of the snaffle bit, a short lunge, and lunge whip with a short strap.

He puts the horse into the *rassembler*, advancing at the walk, halt, rein back, and interrupts at the extremities, giving sugar and caresses. He faces the shoulder of the horse, vibrates the lunge and gives the cadence with the lunging-whip on the inside hock. He alternates the work at the walk and at the shortened trot until be obtains a well-marked diagonalization. He insists on the need of having the horse straight on the outside rein when not going around him on a volte or in shoulder-in. The outside rein is always dominant.

He rides the horse twice around the track at a walk, reins long, then adjusts the reins, goes into sitting trot, cadenced on voltes and inside tracks, then into rising trot and extended trot.

The horse is *ramené* but light. He continues at the trot with the shoulder-in on each rein, executes half-passes as he leaves the center line and extends at the rising trot.

He does counter-changes of hand, holding the haunches at the departure slightly in front of the shoulders.

Again, he takes up haunches-in, haunches-in on half-voltes, returns to the track, croup to the wall. Then the walk on long reins.

Then canter transitions from trot, circle, halts on the circle, transitions on the other rein. Comes back to an extended trot. Now a serpentine at the canter with a few trot strides between each loop, to take off again on the other lead. He does counter-canter. The horse refuses and defends himself a little. Volte at the canter then lead change on the figure of eight. Free walk on long reins.

Lateral transfer from right to left

49. Letter

"Thank you for your letter. I am sending you some photos of horses of different breeds. There are neither breeds that are easy nor difficult. There are horses with heart, strength, good equilibrium, and good movement. You can find these qualities in any breed. There are English Thoroughbreds who are like sardines and do not have the strength to carry the weight of a rider. There are others who are very well balanced. There are Iberian horses that are very over-excited, very nervous, totally lacking gaits. Those are the most difficult ones I have ridden, for they add to their usual difficulties, a hypersensitive disposition and often a lack if strength.

Work with a Thoroughbred at the canter is ridiculously easy, whereas with an Andalusian, one must be an *écuyer* to achieve lead changes at tempo.

Write to me about [William] Steinkrauss' visit to your place." (American world champion in show jumping.)

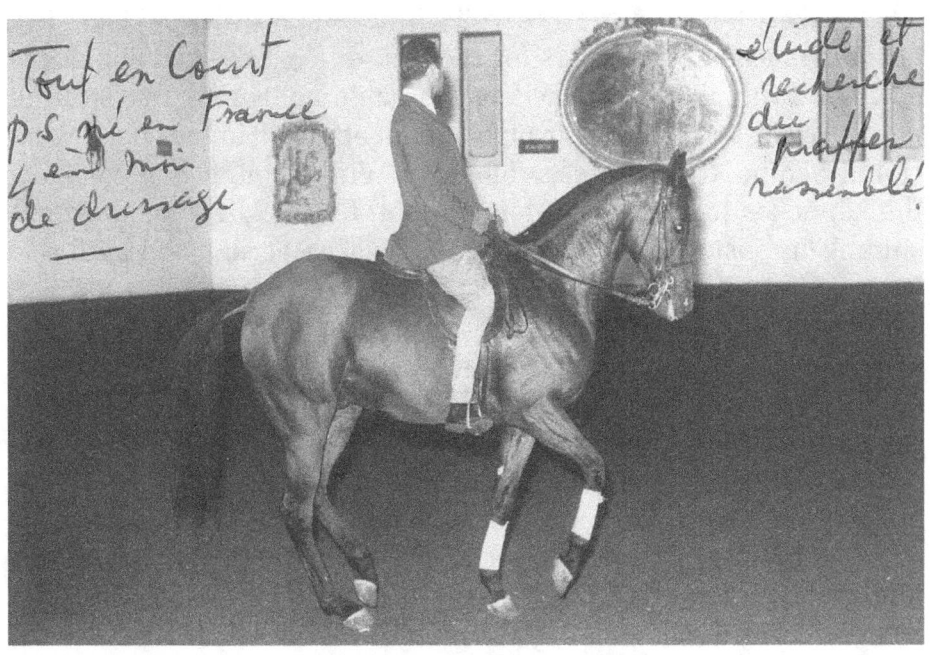

***Tout en Court*, pure English thoroughbred, fourth month in training, in pursuit of piaffe**

50. Note: WORK IN HAND

Shoulder-in with a snaffle. Nuno Oliveira holds the horse almost perpendicular to the long side, then leaves the track, turning the haunches around the shoulders, and then bringing them back to the track. He continues in this fashion around the *manège* with halts, rein backs, keeping the neck rather low. The whip takes the role of the inside leg, is placed on the flank and intervenes with vibrations when the haunches resist. The inside hand vibrates on the inside rein if the shoulders or the neck resist in bending. He turns on the quarter line taking the same position after having passed the first corner, then again rotates the shoulders around the haunches, while going forward. The role of the outside rein is essential here, as it is when mounted. It holds the shoulders, limiting the bend of the neck, regulates impulsion and after having, for example, turned on the center line, it reverses the bend to go on to the half-pass. The horse currently worked wears fairly loose side-reins. According to Nuno it is used to limit excessive bending of the neck.

Then he gives the horse its first lesson at the pillars. The horse is placed at the pillars for the first time, at the halt shoulders level with the pillars. On each side, an aide holds the lunges of the padded cavesson, passed through but not attached to the rings. Nuno stands behind, to the horse's right side. With the lunge whip he gets the haunches to move from left to right, from right to left without shifting his position. This occurs in a state of great calm and the horse is rewarded with some lumps of sugar.

The following day, after a brief preparation in hand, Nuno gets on the horse. At the walk, he again takes up all the movements that had been accomplished in hand. He does a maximum of yieldings of the hand as soon as the horse yields to his demands. Again, he takes up a very perpendicular shoulder-in with a pronounced *ramener* and engaged haunches; he then yields with the hand as he goes forward.

Should contraction occur at the mouth and poll: vibrations followed by a semi-tension. He extends the walk, takes him in again if there is any rushing and goes into the half-pass. The same work at the trot with extended strides, then, with one more extension, he goes into a canter, circles and returns to trot. Shoulder-in at the trot, leg-yield, barely bent on the diagonal.

51. Letter: ACADEMIC EQUITATION OF THE ELDERS

"I have just received your two letters. Now let us see what I have to tell you again on the classical equitation of the elders [authors of past times.]

1. The gaits of these low-built Thoroughbreds that are too extended and brush close to the ground, such as one imagines and admires today, are in conflict with the goal of obtaining a good arrangement of the joints of the horses' limbs which alone enables an equitation on the haunches.

The concept of beauty in *Haute École* equitation varies today according to the schools and the riders.

Which is more beautiful: an Iberian horse who executes the passage and the piaffe up high and *rassemblé* or a thoroughbred executing lead changes at tempo?

Academic equitation of the elders was an art that entailed finesse and harmony and could express the classical airs thanks to the physical conformation of their horses. It was their configuration that made it possible for them to work totally relaxed due to their horses' natural *rassembler*; that is why their riders could work them without forcing a position upon them, which is the *sine qua non* condition to balance horses in order to achieve maximum brilliance and lightness.

Why was Fillis astonished when the engravings of the elders showed horses executing difficult airs well *rassemblés* without any apparent action on the part of the rider's legs? You know the answer.

Our Iberian horses do not run as fast as the others because they are made to turn and move in all directions at the least indication of the seat.

This is the case with *Corsario* who would never allow me to move my foot in the stirrup. These are the horses suitable for equestrian art.

I must look at an Alter [Real] horse for you. I will let you know if he is suitable after I have tried him out."

Nuno Oliveira on Florido, Lusitano, *mise en main*

52. Letter: BE AN ARTIST, NOT A FIGHTER

"My very dear Michel, be an artist and not a fighter! If you are shocked by my article when I say that the Romans were barbarians, that they copied the Greeks but without retaining their subtlety, I allow you to eliminate this, although it is the truth. You will understand the remaining tenor of the article later, when you will have felt certain things riding and working your *Florido*.

Purchase the recording of Fauré's Requiem, lower the light in your *manège*, remain alone without any spectator and begin working *Florido* at a shortened and cadenced trot and at the simple and pure gaits.

I am sure that thereafter, you, who are a sensitive and gentle person, will feel that combat is not the origin of equestrian art.

In equestrian art one feels like weeping with emotion. In combat one cries out of rage and fear. There is quite a difference.

Florido, Professor da Costa's horse, and the *Palha* horse of José Athayde, all very subtle, are horses not suited for combat. The great bullfighter, Joao Nunçio, did not want *Florido*! The mental make-up of these horses was too delicate, they are artistic instruments.

General L'Hotte had good reason to forbid the "bi-corns" [those wearing a two-cornered hat] of the Cadre Noir of Saumur the practice of transcendent equestrian art.

In the past, I, like you, was convinced about all these things. My enormous experience of so many years, my reflections night and day, almost 24 hours a day, have already convinced me of feelings you yourself will arrive at by working and advancing with *Florido*.

I am happy to have been able to find him for you. He is not a horse one schools! Horses like this cannot be "schooled." One must get on their back delicately and try to take advantage of everything that nature has given them. I am happy to see you ride him.

One can teach the technique of equestrian art as I have done to many pupils who are decent chaps and meticulous riders whom I like. One cannot teach this spirit, which many do not have, and Professor Jaime da Costa possesses. He is born with this genius; one finds it in his work. I can give him technical pointers; that is all. You are a man who is endowed with this special mind set, feel with less technique and *Florido* will make you pass through the door of

Nuno Oliveira with *Farista*, Alter Real in piaffe.

equestrian art.

You wrote to José Athayde that you liked my presentation in Brussels, but that it lacked preparation and that I seemed as though I was taking a harmonious walk in this enormous arena. I had tried the rectangle [riding arena] but I lacked air: *Farsista* was able to demonstrate his lightness and spirit in the immense jumping arena!

Equestrian art is like that, appreciate and savor with the noble horse moments of brilliance and precision. I am sure that *Florido* has such a temperament and that you will achieve what I envisage for you in Equitation."

53. Note

CURIOSO, A FOUR YEAR-OLD ALTER REAL
WITH SIX MONTHS OF SCHOOLING

After a few moments of working in hand, bringing the horse in hand [*mise en main*] and putting him at the *rassembler*, the master mounts him and puts him into shoulder-in, at the walk, on a circle on each rein, to prepare for two or three steps of half-pass. Nuno returns to shoulder-in, then half-pass and executes ordinary and reversed pirouettes, while advancing somewhat.

All these movements are approached with a minimum of *rassembler* at the walk and trot.

He then departs at the canter and after some turns and circles he executes a half-volte with haunches-in at the end of the track, returning to the track in half-pass, continues on the track at half-pass, croup to the wall [haunches-out.]

Ansioso at the walk. After doing shoulder-in on the long sides, in both directions, he returns doing half-passes on the center line of the arena. He then turns down the center line and executes a half-pirouette at each end.

Haunches-in on the long sides, a half-pirouette and croup to the wall [haunches-out.] He does almost all of these exercises again at the trot with half-passes on half-diagonals and changes of rein on both tracks.

At the canter a half volte at the end of the track, half-pass, change of lead as he arrives at the wall, on each rein. He goes into a cadenced trot then slows down, halts, puts the horse in *rassembleré* in place. He goes off again at the *doux* passage. He remarks to me that at the walk as at the canter, one tightens the pirouettes to the left less than to the right for, to the left, horses already have a tendency of bending too much, thus [the need for] tightening the outside rein.

When the horse turns his poll towards the outside when doing a half-pass, he is defending himself on the inside of the bit. One must then retake him on the snaffle rein on the inside and on the curb rein on the outside ["division of the contacts" according to Baucher.]

54. Letter

At the Wembley Horse Show, Nuno Oliveira presented *Curioso* several times in front of five thousand people and the royal family. *Curioso* had belonged to a young girl for two years who had used him for riding outdoors. In September 1965 Nuno, bought him back to present him in London in 1966.

His friends and I tried to dissuade him from bringing out a horse that had only twelve months of schooling, even though he was remarkable for... only twelve months of dressage! But having no another horse at the time, he accepted the English invitation. The presentation could not include all the classical airs after such short training, but was noted for some superb moments, and some inevitable gaps.

Articles were complimentary while mixed with reproaches, and our own reserved attitude often put Nuno, similarly in a state of tension. He considered the reactions as a lack of discernment on the part of the critics and an injustice for not having taken into account the difficult conditions he had faced. Lacking finances, he sold quickly, yet skillfully, his well-schooled horses. We saw him almost throughout his whole life in this situation.

"My very dear Michel,

"Those articles that say anything they want, forget to say that the crowds applauded me, as you were able to observe during the last two days when you were there.

I know that you reproach me for having taken out a horse with eleven months of schooling, but my *Curioso* is considerably more perfect than most of these horses in competition that have undergone ten years of schooling.

Could N.,C. K. and others ride a figure eight with lead changes at tempo, do similar transitions, piaffe and passage, and what *rejoneador* [bullfighting horse] could, as *Curioso* did, depart at an extended canter towards the gate with three successive pirouettes?

They write and talk too much and show nothing. It is the enthusiasm of the spectators that interests me and not the hazy theories.

The large public was sensitive and expressed it with their applause. You cannot imagine the number of letters I received from England and also from promoters who are asking me to return in two years.

Forgive me and receive my affection.

P.S. Remember that when horses have years of schooling, they are not better, only routinized and lazy."

55. Note: RIDING THREE ALTER REAL HORSES

I ride the *maître's* three Alter Real horses and he asked me to keep them at a maximum *rassembler*, which causes me great anguish for if it is in this equilibrium that one does one's best work. It is also when one can fail and that horses are the most vulnerable to our mistakes.

These horses are maintained in their original and natural temperament, that is to say, supple, generous, and reactive to the point of excitement. Nuno has retained all of these things, but it is channeled, controllable and usable.

The slightest involuntary movement of the leg unbalances the horse's gait, and involuntary hand movements provoke immediate jolts.

When doing half-passes, Nuno asks me to use simple diagonal effects with the inside leg relaxed and the outside spur placed in contact with the hair, and bending the neck by playing with the fingers of the inside hand without the slightest traction which could provoke right away the throwing out of the haunches on the same side.

Because of their sensitivity and schooling, I ride them right away with the curb reins in my left hand, index and middle finger placed on the right rein to make the bend to the right more thorough.

At lead changes he recommends a moderate use of the hand, simply to change the contact by the action of the fingers, and nothing more. It is essential to always prepare with an increase in impulsion and cadence, before asking for the lead change.

He makes me take a slight bend on the side where the horse canters and right up to the lead changes asks me to maintain cadence with the opposite leg. To change the lead, I very slightly reverse the bend and go on the other leg and, I might say, on the other ischium [seat bone] to provoke the lead change and maintain the cadence.

To go into the piaffe, passage and in general, to obtain gaits at the *rassembler*, of course with horses already quite advanced, one must always begin by giving impulsion through tension in the [rider's] back and seat, vibrate with the legs, eventually a touch with the spur.

Then, almost simultaneously, one must bring the horse in hand, and once everything falls together, yield the hand and leg, replaced by the tension of the seat, without the horse modifying either his equilibrium or his carriage.

At the outset of the trot, the *maître* asks me to do a slight half-halt on the left rein, the right rein holding the neck straight, whether I am tracking right or left.

Simultaneously, flexion of the left knee which brings the leg [calf] to the rounded part of the belly, and the passage is launched.

To go from the passage to the piaffe, one does the same maneuver but with a more pronounced, more "slowing" half-halt, then immediately a yielding of the hand, lumbars arched, playing imperceptibly with the legs and keeping the diagonalization almost in place.

Riding the very subtle Alter horses of the *maître*, the rhythmic feeling and their suppleness is impressive.

He has me approach some voltes at the trot, alternating between haunches-in and shoulder-in and from there, extensions on the long side. Preparation for extension is done through the confirmation of the *rassembler*, a little jab with both legs which then remain fixed, holding and advancing the hands somewhat, upper body slightly back.

At the canter he has me execute a volte at the counter-canter and as I come out of the volte, link on another volte simply to prepare for the pirouettes.

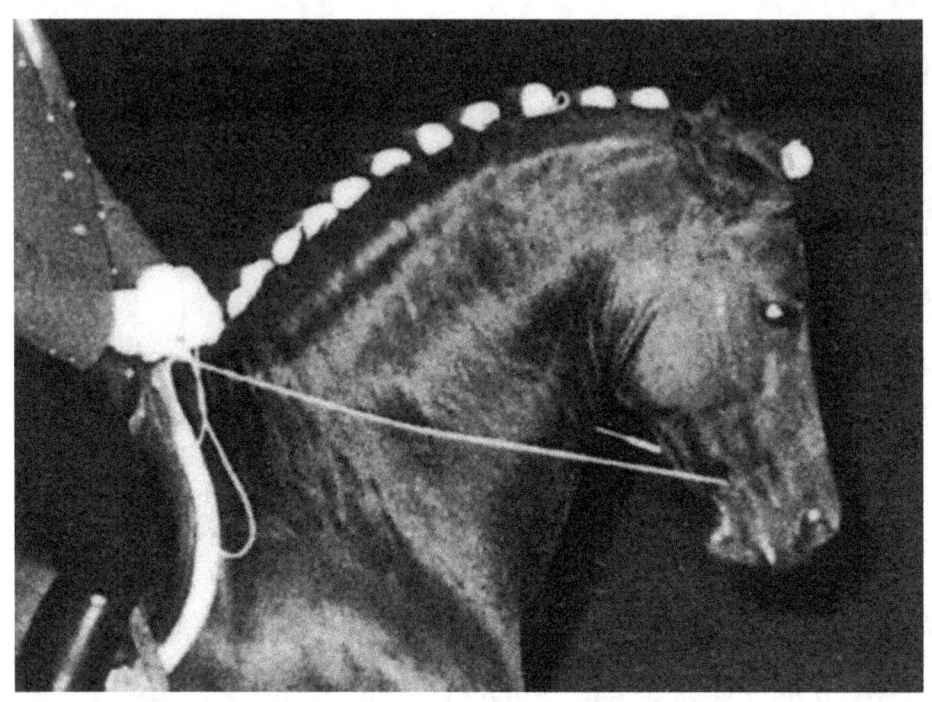

Corsario, Alter Real, in passage *"sur le fil."* (detail) ("on the thread.") [Note the lack of bridle; Nuno holds only thin white cord as reins, no bit.]

Corsario, Alter Real, in passage *"sur le fil"*

56. Letter

Nuno writes to me to talk about an official presentation at the *Palais Royal de la Nécessidade* in Lisbon, at which the highest authorities of the Portuguese Government will be present.

It is precisely his Alter horses which he will present in the company of his pupil Don José Athayde, at the time *écuyer* at the Alter Stud farm.

He draws technical reflections from his rehearsals, which always tangent the philosophical sphere. He suggests that I adopt this as an example for a book I am writing, but without quoting him.

"My dear Michel,

I am very busy directing the rehearsals at the *Nécessidade*. After working with my horses from 5 a.m. on, I go there at 10 a.m. where I remain until 5 p.m. and return to my *manège* for the evening lessons.

Corsario does wonderful work. It is a pleasure to ride him. I rode *Brioso* for José who listens to me diligently and I believe that he will do very well. *Ansioso* is always very brilliant and Christiane is very good with *Aljezur*.

With respect to your book, you must absolutely consider writing: True lightness, the one that encompasses the ensemble of the horse, from his mouth to his back, produces a cadence and a communication which increases the pleasure of riding.

It is a sensation which is a true secret conversation between the horse and yourself and from which the spectator only perceives the gracefulness. Nobody can appreciate the rest; only horse and rider know what is going on.

I shall give you an example which you will not quote but perhaps you may find a similar one. The other day, in the *manège de la Nécessidade,* there were some electricians working on an aluminum ladder and making a lot of noise with their equipment. *Brioso* and *Aljezur* who are much calmer than *Corsario*, reacted by getting off the bit and spinning around to escape. Neither reins nor legs could make them go past the workers. On the other hand, *Corsario* trembled, but it sufficed for me to lean my torso slightly back to confirm his *rassembler* and he passed the ladder, ears pointed forward.

My son Joao, who was there, remarked to me that the other horses did not have a sufficient *rassembler*, due to a lack of lightness, and could therefore not be completely restrained. It is the *rassembler* of *Corsario* which put him at my disposition. Do not quote this example, but think about it so that you can write about it. Also speak about true impulsion which produces feline gestures rather than jerks. Also be inspired, without quoting me, by the perfection of the impulsion in his extended trot and school canter.

If your horse *Damasco* becomes annoyed when you *rassembler* him and instead gives you movements that are high and rushed rather than forward, do not worry about it. With the utmost delicacy, do combinations of shoulder-in on voltes and half-passes, haunches-in, in an attempt to have the horse accept frequent yielding of the hand. Do all this, while maintaining the spurs on the coat, caressing the flanks, and which are actions that allow yieldings of the hand.

I assure you that at the end of a week you will write to me saying that you are having good results.

Do not become impatient, for *Damasco* is your best horse, albeit, the most complicated one. Be aware of one thing, I have never worked *Corsario* at the ample gaits and yet, over there [at the *manège de la Nécessidade*], in the large *manège*, it is he who extends the best, in a most flowing and easy manner, at the trot and canter.

The *rassembler* and the lightness that emerge from the true *rassembler* give you everything.

Should your horse lower his head slightly and place it behind the vertical, do not worry. It is a phase wherein he is seeking his definitive position in which his haunches are totally flexed. When he does that, then he will position himself well.

No rider can solve the problems of over-excitation, laziness, lack of lightness, or the rigidity of school gaits through extensions. With this system you tense your horse the German way [tension against the hand] and that is not what we are seeking. Bend your horse constantly on voltes and tight exercises and profit from these flexions by constant yielding with the hand.

Do not forget what I have just told you."

Nuno Oliveira and *Invencivel*, Lusitano, pesade.

57. Note

To obtain the *effet d'ensemble* [combined effect] one extends the upper body while approaching the body of the horse with the legs lightly, then the spurs, raising the wrists to arrive at an equal [on both reins] contact with the mouth.

One can prepare the piaffe with long reins which is a question of skill and a preparation that precedes the long reins.

The curb bit must be placed two fingers below the snaffle [in the horse's mouth.]

Preparing for impulsion and the *rassembler* with an extension of the trot in mind, among other ways, one must put a semi-bend to the shoulder-in before reaching the corner preceding the extension, then straighten with the outside rein and by giving a slap with both legs which then remain immobile.

To piaffe from the passage. Lower the hands, fingers closed to provoke the slowing down of the passage and lowering of the neck. Keep hands very quiet and slide the relaxed legs somewhat backwards.

One must not piaffe using one's heels.

Horses over bend either due to a rigid hand [pulling on the reins], or due to a lack of impulsion. Often due to both causes.

THE *MAÎTRE* WORKS A FOUR-AND-A-HALF YEAR OLD

He asks for a shoulder-in at 40 degrees in relation to the wall. He holds his hands high on the snaffle rein to prevent the horse from over-flexing, and then returns to the four reins. The young horse opens his mouth and takes a hesitant step. He puts him into a rather high-stepping trot with impulsion on a volte at the shoulder-in, then "unrolls" him [the horse's body is extended longitudinally] by means of a very spectacular extension.

He interrupts this work with half-passes on the diagonal. He does not hesitate to give quick little vibrations with the hand held high if the horse changes his position or lowers his neck abruptly.

At the canter, the hands must always be held quite high, giving little vibrations when the horse lowers his head and neck abruptly.

LESSON AT THE SPANISH TROT ON *CORSARIO*, AN ALTER REAL, WHO IS ALREADY AT THE PASSAGE, PIAFFE, AND SPANISH WALK

Nuno asks me for repeated *jambettes* in the rhythm of the passage with a slight bend on the side of the foreleg asked.

The *jambette* is obtained through a pronounced diagonal effect. It is executed on the same side, on one or several turns around the *manège,* and then repeated in the other direction.

'For my dear Michel, This Spanish trot of *Corsario* is performed without tension and in a joyous *rassembler*" 1967

It should be noted that the horse is only doing the basic movements of the Spanish walk; however, he ends by doing three strides of the Spanish trot in the rhythm of the passage.

Mounted, during this lesson, I gesticulate [move the hands] too much and put the horse out of balance. I must slide my legs further back and indicate with the aid of semi-taut reins. Go forward again with the help of the two spurs.

58. Letter: *FLORIDO'S* EXCITEMENT

This letter is in answer to my concerns with respect to questions about *Florido's* considerable excitement. This horse,

Nuno Oliveira on *Florido*, Lusitano schooling passage

of exceptional type, had several times unseated his breeder, once during an annual breed show. Sold to a bullfighter who had never been able to accustom him to training exercises dealing with bulls, he then sold him to me. One could not get near his legs without him going into *lançades* [forward leaps] or furious half-pirouettes.

"I did, indeed, receive your letter. It is absolutely essential that you insist until your horse becomes orderly under your command, in his *rassembler*, and in his lightness.

Settle your buttocks well into the saddle, stabilize your knees and hold yourself straight, shoulders above your hips. See to it that the action of your legs is correct and gentle and, above all, immobile. You must be able to reach the point when the contact of your spurs manages to calm the horse by means of the *effet d'ensemble*.

If he becomes even more over-excited, continue insisting until he becomes perfectly calm. I did, indeed, observe your *Florido* when I rode him. I am sure that you will never obtain lead changes without the *rassembler*, thus in a state of calm, you must give him this lesson before going further.

Please read the little book by Victor Franconi [1810-1897 riding teacher of King Louis-Philippe's children; private riding master of Napoléon III; director of the Cirque d'hiver; employer of F. Baucher] in the chapter devoted to lead changes.

From this lesson you will obtain not only calmness and the *rassembler* at lead changes, but it will help you with the[*mise en main*] at the walk and the trot by making your horse rounder, which he has not yet become. He still lengthens his neck too much, which prevents the *rassembler* of the highest order.

Mix all this with a free extended canter, but round!

Forgive me for insisting, but with this horse you must obtain an exceptional result and not an average one!"

59. Note

NUNO OLIVEIRA GIVES A LESSON RIDING MY HORSES *DAMASCO* AND *CRUZADO*

After a brief period of relaxation, regular halts from the walk, transitions to *trot rassemblé*, regular halts. From the halt, three or four steps at the rein back, return to walk, then from rein back to trot.

Shoulder-in on the track on one side, haunches-in on the other end with a half-pirouette before reaching the corner and return to the track, croup to the wall.

This sequence of exercises at the walk and the trot, later at the canter, is La Guérinière's basic lesson. Then, transitions from shoulder-in to haunches-in on circles at the walk and trot.

From a *trot rassemblé,* do a few strides of passage, followed again by a *trot rassemblé*.

Work at the canter on circles, spirals, half-voltes, and counter-canter. Depart from a halt on the circle to counter-canter and on a half-volte haunches-in which prepare the pirouettes.

With respect to *Cruzado* who is very cold-blooded, add many extensions at the trot and half-passes on the diagonal, up the center line, then extensions, especially at the trot.

For a phlegmatic horse, give a few "small *attaques*" with the spurs, barely touching with the legs but using one's calves. "Animate" for as long as possible with these "*attaques*" without moving the haunches.

60. Letter

"After my return to Lisbon I took up my work at the *manège* again, happy to find my horses once more and everything else here that is dear to me.

I was satisfied with your horses' progress and to see that in *Damasco* you have a wonderful horse.

It is true, my dear Michel, that *Haute École* equitation is only possible with very good horses. But we learn a great deal with the others. One can even school them to the point that they can do everything, but it will never be great music.

Do you think that it would have been possible to have the success I have had with *Curioso* without his natural equilibrium and lightness? Of course, I have a certain kind of equestrian tact but the horse is especially gifted.

Do you think that I could have taught him those wonderful pirouettes had he not been a horse of quality? And his lead changes are so good because his natural canter is very good. One can teach lead changes to almost any horse, but not all have this wonderful movement. What counts in equitation is not to collect all the various airs but to obtain that equilibrium which will give the horse his true lightness.

This is in accordance with my study of the principles of Monsieur de La Guérinière and the *écuyers* of his school.

Then it was the period of Baucher, Fillis, and all the others who were delighted to be able to execute the complicated airs, the backwards canter, or the canter on three legs. Would they have been able to canter freely with a good cadence after a pirouette or a series of flying changes at tempo?

I believe, my dear Michel that it is in this vein that we must search and work. You are one of those rare *écuyers* capable of riding with intelligence and you will have good results."

61. Note

THE MASTER WORKS WITH *CORIOLANO*

He is six years old, has already been worked by the breeder and now for ten days by Oliveira.

At the walk he does the shoulder-in on tight voltes together with pirouettes to supple the horse. At the first contraction, he stops him.

From the shoulder-in he goes on to the half-pass, but as soon as the horse resists, he goes back to the shoulder-in. During these exercises he multiplies light *effets d'ensemble* to relax him. He prepares the trot through the *effet d'ensemble* at the walk and with little touches of the spur to obtain lightness and maintain it at the trot.

At the end of the lesson he dismounts, takes the horse by the hand on the curb-rein, holding his head and neck very low, then, with a short lunging-whip, he asks him two or three strides of piaffe.

62. Letter

NUNO'S REFLECTIONS:

"The horsemen of the past worked their horses with a great concern for obtaining accentuated bend on voltes and lateral work. Today's horsemen want them straighter, thereby, reducing the possibility of suppleness and lightness. For me, easy lateral mobility is essential and occurs before the crossing.

Small *attaques* [with the spurs] at the three gaits, in perfect accord with the hand, at a certain stage, are indispensable. An immobile hand, fingers light, must have beneficial effects of which the main one is the improvement of the *rassembler*, stabilizing it, and what emerges from it: balance and lightness. Give free [light] jabs when yielding with the hand and firm jabs with a fixed hand.

Free jabs prepare the horse to accept firm *attaques*. After a poorly given jab or after he has become excited, the horse can rush the gait. This must definitely be stopped: by a supple and open seat, immobile hands and legs, halts, rein backs, then to move on once again only with the seat, at a semi-shoulder-in and a slightly extended trot.

A shoulder-in at the canter opposes the equilibrium, but is favorable to its suppling. It must only be asked when the horse is sufficiently advanced at the canter, counter-canter, and half-passes at the canter.

It is very important at the beginning of the pirouettes, to be satisfied with the bend on the counter-shoulder-in. Searching for the correct bend, especially on the left side where it risks being excessive, could easily make the horse feel cornered when the head faces his haunch!

Important - When a young horse has difficulties executing the half-pass on whatever rein:

1) Should he resist, reverse the bend in the neck which puts him into a shoulder-in.

2) Take him back to the shoulder-in when the half-pass becomes difficult.

3) Take him back to the shoulder-in on the opposite side.

4) Take advantage of the bend of the shoulder-in to execute, at the end of the track [corner], a rotation on the haunches with the bend of the half-pass, continuing delicately on to a half-pass on the diagonal."

63. Letter

In this letter, interesting remarks are made with respect to the English Thoroughbred who in 1975, still represented dressage horses, except in Germany. Critical reflection based on draw-reins and finally some cutting remarks which none of us ever escaped and which was part of his singular and difficult temperament.

The last section of the letter is one of those capital executions to which he had the secret and which he always reserved, curiously, for those who were closest to him in equitation and friendship.

Nuno Oliveira on *Ousado*, Lusitano, passage. Lima, Peru.

"I have been in Peru for twenty days now working ten hours a day. I am resting a bit today and writing to you. Riding all these Thoroughbreds here, I thought of you and your Thoroughbred that I like very much. They are very sensitive and nervous horses and even if they appear cold [non-reactive], it is basically that they are contracted [rigid] in the head.

With your horse, at first, force him as little as possible, do not push him too much. Try to relax his mind and I think you will have a valuable horse.

Draw-reins are perhaps acceptable for German horses whose temperament and conformation are rigid and heavy with strong necks and with the backs of carriage horses. But, they are bad for horses that are sensitive and hot.

The German rider here in Lima abuses the draw-reins. They gave his horses rigid backs with forced *rameners* which do not correspond to their conformation. I worked a great deal trying to supple these horses, but some were already so rigid that everything one does is useless.

I have to leave for Costa Rica after-tomorrow for a week and then I return home right away.

Madame Phyllis Field bought from me the Anglo-Arab you had ridden and I bought an extraordinary *"Ervideira"* [a Portuguese bloodline founded in 1888] at the Golega Fair.

The performance at Golega was sad and unfortunately my pupils and friends were there. "X." on a grey horse, completely rigid. "Y.", the good, "Y." with one of *Pluto's* sons who is a well of contractions. "Z." very happy with himself, walking majestically with his horse, twisted and stubborn [hostile], legs wide apart, a huge bit in his mouth, doing I don't know what kind of Baucherist movements. My foreign pupils, who were with me, were astonished.

Equitation is a marvelous art, but only if one does not remain in a state of mediocrity.

64.   Note: LETTER FROM JEAN-CLAUDE MENUT

Here is a letter I received from a young Frenchman from Lisbon, Jean-Claude Menut, a pleasant chap and a good rider, who had previously worked with me for a year. He is an *écuyer* in Manila. He recounts here the twelfth training session given by Nuno Oliveira to a five year-old English Thoroughbred.

"Nuno begins with work in hand, mobilizing the haunches around himself on voltes, then on the track in shoulder-in. He does a few flexions in hand, while moving forward. His first groom, Abel accompanies him with a lunge whip to maintain the forward movement. Nuno relaxes the jaw by placing the end of his whip near it, remarking that it is a procedure by [Captain] Raabe.

Mounted work: At the walk he seeks a regular cadence, straight and at the shoulder-in. He reminds me that it is being executed according to La Guérinière. Then counter shoulder-in, then half turns on the haunches, which are almost pirouettes, while going forward, then head to the wall with a successful attempt at diagonalization. He does very correct half-passes and counter-changes of hand.

At the trot - He does circles with a lateral effect, followed by a shoulder-in on the track, then the same thing, changing rein. Finally, he executes voltes on two tracks with a lateral effect."

THE MASTER SAYS TO ME: [This is still Menut's letter to Henriquet]
"1) The horse is trying to find his equilibrium. The *Haute École* airs are only for the amusement of the *écuyer* when he has his horse balanced. I point out to you a lead change at an extended canter which the master asked "just to see."
2) One hand or one leg must not be used in isolation but always compensated by the effect of the other hand and leg.
3) One must alternate the outside and inside rein on the circle. This is a good exercise."

The horses of the master are making astounding progress. He insisted that I [Menut] report this to you, and even wanted me to mail the letter that very evening! After this very praiseworthy effort to write, I leave you to return to my horses.

65. **Note:** WORK IN HAND WITH *CORIOLANO*, 8 MONTHS OF SCHOOLING

Shoulder-in on tight voltes and from there, reversing the bend of the neck, placing shoulders in front of haunches and executing half-passes. To do this, Nuno holds one hand near the snaffle, the other in the middle of the reins and takes the horse forward in half-passes towards the track where he puts him at the *rassembler* with the aid of the whip (which is in his hand placed in the middle of the reins) and asks him to piaffe.

More work in hand with an Alter Real horse which has only two months of schooling. He has him move forwards and backwards, and has an aide assist him who stands at the horse's haunches.

REMARKS MADE BY THE MASTER

"How can one prevent a young horse from being crooked at the canter without using too much hand and leg?

One must do multiple voltes and go into the counter-canter in order to profit from the *manège* wall to straighten and guide the horse. When one returns to the true canter one must increase impulsion which straightens the haunches.

How can one extend the trot? *Rassembler* and cadence the horse on the snaffle, with leg vibrations. Arch the [rider's] lumbars, not the dorsals, give a slap with the legs, stabilize them, and allow them to slacken. The hand must not leave the contact, but pick up and measure the impulsion.

To obtain extension at the trot, if the action of the two legs near the horse is not sufficient, touch with the spur, allow the neck to be lowered into the hand. The neck must not be raised again.

For the Spanish trot, the procedure is the same, with the same position, but the rider's legs are more forward.

For the canter transitions, simply approach the opposite leg against the coat until touching with the spur if necessary, without jabbing and at the same time hold the inside leg at the girth."

66. Letter: TONGUE CONCERNS

I was extremely concerned when, in the presence of the *maître* on several occasions during work, I noticed the tongue of a horse appear outside its mouth. This occurred for no other reason than when executing lateral work without any force. I can say today that this horse, which was then about five years old, ceased this habit the following month.

"Thank you for your letter. I was very happy during my visit at your place.

With respect to your horse's tongue: put your snaffle as high as possible and hold your hand very quiet. Each time you feel that the tongue is not where it should be, execute some voltes at a medium trot, maintaining your horse on a perfect circumference around your inside leg, pushing with the top of the calf from back to front in a movement that goes together with that of the horse's flank.

Quite obviously you have to ride the horse with a simple snaffle, with the nose band in front of the bit [dropped nose band]; adjusted but not tight. The more you perfect the horse's self-carriage and his impulsion, the better you will solve this problem.

Rare are the horses with this problem that must be ridden somewhat earlier with a curb and snaffle bit; I repeat, they are rare.

When your horse really bends his sides, he will no longer have this problem with his tongue. Tongue problems are always due to contractions and rigidity when one does lateral movements.

Be sure that the bend on the rigid side when doing voltes is maintained by the action of the leg, as I told you, rather than by the inside rein which in this case, must be less taut than the outside rein.

In total friendship."

67: Note: A STUDY OF PIAFFE IN HAND AND MOUNTED

After the horse has been correctly brought in hand [*mise en main*], walking straight, do a halt that is *rassemblé*, rein back and transition, halt, walk, trot. Tracking left, hold the curb and snaffle reins in the left hand 15 cm from the bits, and hold the whip in the right hand, placing oneself facing the horse's shoulder.

Execute the shoulder-in at the walk, then at the trot on a volte touching the track; when arriving on the track, straighten the horse with the right outside rein and take advantage of the dancing cadence to steal from him a few piaffe-like walk steps [*quelque pas piaffé.*] Encourage him with the whip at the flank and at the slightest diagonalization reward him and stop for a few minutes.

In the study of the piaffe in hand, as well as mounted, one must go forward quite a bit and be content with one or two strides in place and resume the forward movements. For this purpose, use the whip at the haunches, and to go forward, tap on the saddle or on the horse's back.

MOUNTED PIAFFE

To take on the piaffe, start at the walk, progressively shortening, going from normal strides to strides of 20 to 30 cm without the horse halting. Keep his neck low and ask for diagonalization in place only when lightness occurs and through a light flexion alternated with each knee. The horse must be rounded when these actions occur, form a ball by raising his back, engaging his haunches and keeping the neck rather low at the beginning. He will then give active piaffe-like steps.

When the horse begins to understand these aids, one can ask for diagonalization by slowing down the *trot rassemblé*. Likewise, from the passage, arriving at the point where the passage contains the piaffe, closing the fingers slowly, imperceptibly advancing the hand and the lumbar muscles, while placing the upper body backwards. It is the tension of the seat going forward that maintains impulsion and not the strong actions of legs and spurs.

THE MASTER MAKES SOME REMARKS

"When you find that some necks break at the base, over-bend or fall backwards and invert, work with the inside snaffle rein and the outside curb rein, give impulsion with the outside leg and limit the bend of the neck.

Also look for extension of the neck, downwards and forwards, with impulsion at the medium trot.

Work with the outside rein, the inside hand limited to fixing the neck straight on straight lines and bent on curves or lateral work.

Think about the cadence of the gaits, and their amplitude. Improve it with light half-halts and combined effects given in cadence and not against the beat.

Impostor, Lusitano in piaffe

68: Note

THE MASTER RIDES TWO HORSES BELONGING TO STUDENTS

The first one has a somewhat mediocre balance, his trot cadence is weak, and his rigidity is obvious. He works him at the walk and trot, multiplying voltes and circles with maximum flexion. The same at the shoulder-in with a pronounced neck bend.

He does halts and frequent rein backs from which he goes into a trot. He changes the horse's position with leg-yield, from the middle of the short side to the middle of the long side and puts him into the *rassembler* when arriving at the track.

He makes him do half-passes on diagonals in counter-bend, at the three gaits. He adds rein backs, diagonalizations, canter transitions and touches somewhat on the passage without a pronounced suspension. The natural cadence of the trot is moderate and the horse makes head movements.

He continues to rein back, brings him forward, diagonalizing from the walk that is *rassemblé* and concludes by rotating the haunches around the shoulders to the right and to the left. He extends at the rising trot.

The four year-old youngster he then rides does not seem to be any more flexible. He puts him right away into the walk at the shoulder-in almost perpendicular [to the wall] and, still at the walk, he begins combinations wherein he alternates the shoulder-in with the half-pass. The horse also throws his head up, so he continues to alternate between the shoulder-in and half-pass without going forward much. To control the head defenses, he recommends bending him well at the walk and on the volte, holding him between the seat and not much hand, on gentle reins, the neck quite low. Nuno insists that one must not let him pull the reins out of the hands. To prevent these head defenses, one must hold one's arms firmly against the body, but without punishing him and without hitting on the horse's mouth. The horse must punish himself by throwing himself at a fixed hand which will force him to stop.

If the hands move and are loose on the reins, it will encourage him to pull them away.

He remarks about the lower aids at the piaffe:

Mark the rhythm by alternately flexing the knees in such a way that the upper part of the leg [calf] comes imperceptibly in contact with the bulging part of the horse's belly at the moment when he places the same diagonal on the ground. This is easily seen when the master works in piaffe.

He then recommends opening the trot, that is to say, to go from a more high-stepping trot, to a trot that is lightly extended, thus open.

Extensions are for later, when the horse has been well positioned in the *rassemblé*.

Coriolano, passage

69. Letter: CORRECTING A LATERALIZED WALK

In this last document, Nuno Oliveira, whom I consulted with respect to the tendency of my two horses to lateralize at the walk when I reduced its amplitude, analyzed the situation and considered all the corrective methods possible.

"I did, indeed, receive your letter yesterday. Here is what I think about this problem.

Let us analyze it. A horse ambles instead of walking correctly for different reasons: lack of impulsion, rigidity of the back, suffering from weak loins, compression between hand and legs.

I believe that in the case of your horse, it is the back that is not yet sufficiently suppled.

Remedies. Work the bends on short voltes, the horse must be well bent toward the inside, with equal contact on the inside rein as on the outside rein (in any case never stronger on the inside rein.)

Ask for the exercise in one direction, followed immediately in the other direction.

As soon as you have felt that the horse has really yielded in his entire body, stop him frequently during the exercise. This means halt him bent to one side, then to the other.

Then verify that he responds with impulsion, walking straight and forward. As soon as he begins to amble again, repeat the preceding exercises.

Other remedies. Start out at the working trot on circles with a great deal of impulsion, bending him and holding his haunches outwards. When you feel that he has really yielded with his haunches, his back is relaxed, the impulsion is calm and cadenced, do the transition to the walk in the same position and become one with the horse, raising the reins to bring the horse in hand [*the mise en main.*]

Take him on a *rassemblé* walk again and as soon as he ambles, go back to the preceding exercises.

Another remedy. At the walk execute voltes with a small diameter, horse well bent, reins must be very long. As soon as you feel that your horse has the whole interior side of his body bent around your inside leg, start all over again with this exercise, but regulate the reins in such a way that the head and neck return to the position they had during the bringing of the horse in hand [*la mise en main*], then continue on straight.

Yet another remedy. Go very slowly at the walk, more and more shortened. Each time he ambles, stop him, rein back two or three steps, stop him, rein back again, go forward at a very slow walk, and so on.

Here, my dear Michel, is what your old friend advises you. Love to Catherine.

Yours,

Nuno"

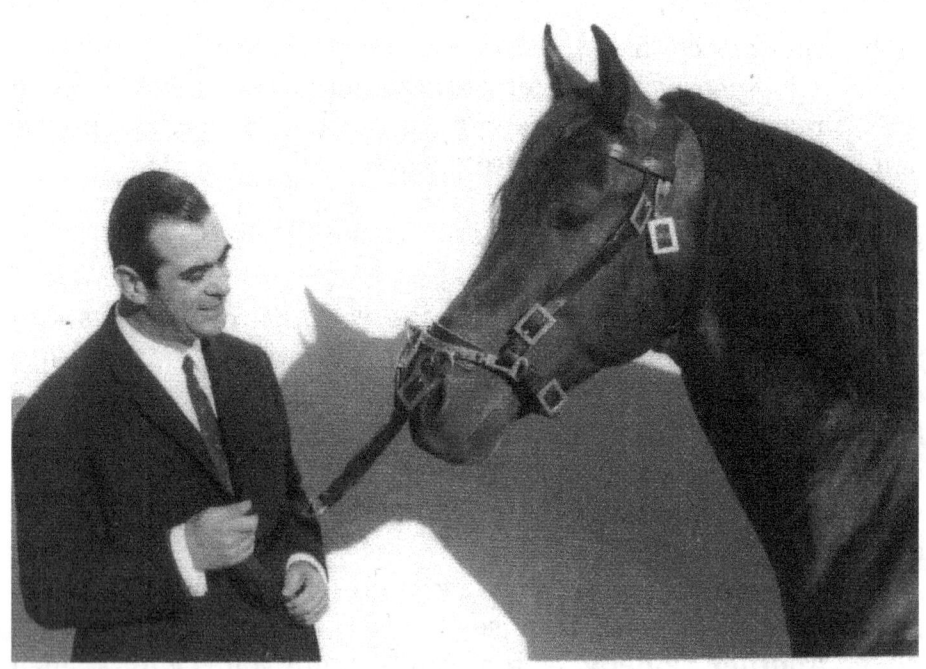

Nuno Oliveira

70:   Letter: NEW YEAR WISHES

To conclude, here is a short letter dated 23 December 1979, wherein the *maître* sends me his best wishes [for the New Year] accompanied by some philosophical reflections as he always liked to do, however, without ever straying from thoughts on equitation.

"Entering the New Year we wish you as much happiness as possible.

In the world of today which changes so rapidly and is so fascinating, we shall see how the horse will survive.

We are told that Europe is in a state of crisis and that it will manage to get out of it. This is not true. The whole world, including the United States, will soon also be in a state of crisis.

After the war, in Western Europe, we became used to living in tremendous comfort and we continue to spend a great deal. Soon we will become aware that this is no longer possible and that the entire world will have to lead a simpler life so that each individual can eat. Individualism is disappearing and, as it is with the ants, it will be the law of the community that will be the *modus vivendi* of the near future.

What will the future bring to the horse, to the half-pass, and the piaffe? They are a luxury, but they are also part of culture.

Do not, however, forget that in China, Mao Tse Tung eliminated horses and dogs for food. Well, perhaps I am wrong. Be that as it may, I continue to do my shoulder-ins any piaffes as well as I can and always with great interest.

With all our friendship,

Nuno and Branca"

GLOSSARY

Half-pass (*Appuyer*) : Exercise in which the horse moves laterally, its head turned in the direction it is going, its body and neck bent in the direction of going.

Attack/Jab/Touch (*Attaque*): Energetic action of the heel or spur.

Circle (*Cercle*): Exercise in which the horse must adapt its bend according to the part of the circumference it is covering.

Yield (*Cession*): Appropriate yielding action of the rider's leg or hand. It is also the relaxation of the horse's poll and jaw upon request.

Lead change (*Changement de pied*): The gesture of the horse changing from canter on the left lead to canter on the right lead and vice versa.

Counter shoulder-in (*Contre epaule-en -dedans*): Variation of the shoulder-in turned towards the wall.

Counter canter, Canter on the outside lead (*Contre-galop*): When the horse is going on the left track but cantering on the right lead and vice versa.

Semi-tension (*Demi-tension*): In traditional classical equitation, where the contact with the snaffle bit is light but permanent; the contact on the curb bit being even more subtle.

Yielding of the hand(s) or leg(s)(*Descente de main ou de jambes*): Voluntary release of the aids, the horse keeping its position and balance intact.

Diagonal (*Diagonale*): Diagonal inside track which goes from one side of the arena to the opposite.

Diagonalisation (*Diagonalisation*): Action in which the horse jumps from one diagonal pair of legs to the other. example: in Piaffe,

Passage. Left hind with right fore, and right hind with left fore.
"Soft" Passage (*Doux Passage*): Intermediary phase within which the horse in training goes from a *rassemblé* trot, to the passage.

Effet d'ensemble: Baucherist expression signifying to enfold the horse between the leg and bit to calm excessive movements. Combined effect.

Shoulder-in (*Epaule en dedans*): Fundamental exercise within which the horse moves laterally on three tracks, harmoniously curved from the poll to the tail.

Gaule: Stick made from birch or quince wood.

Golega: Capital Portuguese village renowned for the breeding of Lusitano horses.

Pigeon throat (*Gorge de pigeon*): Excessive enlargement of the lower part of the neck, resulting from a forced *Ramener*.

Haunches in, Haunches-out (*Hanche en dedans, Hanche en dehors*): First element of the half-pass. The forehand remains straight and parallel to the wall, the hindquarters towards the inside or outside, on three tracks.

Jambette: Maximum elevation of the front leg, preparation for the Spanish walk.

Ambling (*Lateraliser*): Defective gait; The horse walks with the two legs on the same side moving forward together.

Diagonal legs (*Membres diagonaux*): Left front leg associated to the right hind leg and vice versa.

Parrocel, Charles: French painter and engraver, author of the illustrations in *"L'Ecole de cavalerie"* by La Guérinière. [*Ecole de Cavalerie, Part II*, (School of Horsemanship) Xenophon Press 1992]

Passage: Majestic and cadenced diagonalised trot.

Piaffe (*Piaffer*): Diagonalisation in place obtained by the progressive shortening of the walk or passage on the spot.

Plaquer: False attitude of a horse in an excessive ramener; When the horse's jaw is stuck to the base of the neck.

Bend (*Pli*): Bend, more particularly of the neck.

To bend (*Ployer*): To incite the bend of the neck.

Ramener: To put the head and neck as a whole in a position allowing for the *mise en main* (putting the horse on the bit.) The *ramener* is complete when the horse's forehead is almost vertical and the poll the highest point of the cervical vertebrae.

Rassembler: Superior state of balance and collection obtained through the flexibility of the haunches brought forward which in turns, allows for the elevation of the front end.

Renvers: French term used in German equitation to indicate the half-pass along the wall (haunches to the wall)(haunches out.)

Semi-shoulder-in: Shoulder-fore, similar to shoulder-in but with less angle, closer to 10-15 degrees with the path of travel.

Tension/Tautness (*Tension*): Positive tension or tautness is that of the horse on itself. Bad tension or tautness is that of a horse against the rider's hand.

Travers: French term used in German equitation to indicate the half-pass along the wall (head to the wall)(haunches-in.)

Circle, (*Volte*): Circle with a diameter smaller than 10m.

ABOUT THIS BOOK

This classical text, which knowledgeable horsemen have been anxiously awaiting for years, is finally available in English. Henriquet's personal record of correspondence provides a unique window into the private problem-solving dialogue between master and student. Now a master *écuyer* in his own right, Henriquet embellishes this new edition with 50 photographs from his personal collection. This first and only English edition includes many more photographs of Nuno Oliveira and his teacher than earlier editions. This English edition also has been embellished with a glossary and a descriptive table of contents for the 70 chapters.

Michel Henriquet was born in 1924, and held a degree in Law and Letters. In search of elusive traditional classic French equitation, he believed might be lost, Michel Henriquet first studied with the Baucherist, Rene Bacharach, a student of Captain Étienne Beudant [*Horse Training: Outdoors and High School,* Xenophon Press 2014]. Henriquet was among the first admirers of Master Nuno Oliveira, becoming a friend and disciple over thirty years, until the latter's death. Mr. Henriquet passed on December 8, 2014 and is survived by his loving and devoted wife, Catherine Durand Henriquet.

"I inserted between the letters, most of the notes I've ever taken over the years. They are, sometimes the 'screenplay' of what I just saw in the ring. In some cases I have carefully noted the tips and reflections that reveal valuable concepts. Finally, I note the criticisms and comments that the Master sent me regarding a working session. This body of didactic elements reminds all those who have had the opportunity to work with him, most of his philosophy, in its most direct form. And for those who, although have not experienced this instruction first hand, fortunately, it will add to the discovery that they can do by reading about his great work."

—Michel Henriquet.

www.ingramcontent.com/pod-product-compliance
Lightning Source LLC
Chambersburg PA
CBHW050553300426
44112CB00013B/1893